THE
ARTFUL DODGER'S
GUIDE TO PLANNING
YOUR ESTATE

WHAT FOLKS HAVE SAID
ABOUT THIS BOOK:

"This book is a light-hearted examination of estate taxes and the planning to avoid them. If you are in the estate-planning mood, this comical approach might spur your learning in advance of that visit to your own lawyer."

Kent S. Collins, *The Senior Forum*

"Thanks to the wisdom and humor of Hawley, we now not only have a guide to planning our estates, but a chance to understand the process."

Lisa Watson, *The Monterey Herald*

"If all lawyers could write like Thomas Hawley, the profession would benefit immensely. This is the best book I have read since graduating from Boalt in 1949."

William T. Marocllo, Administrative Law Judge (Retired)

"A fact-filled manual that takes the mystery out of the estate planning process, and is a very good read to boot."

Robert Campbell, Mystery Writers
of America Edgar Award Winner

". . . a great source of information for those who need to know how Uncle Sam taxes things and how a good lawyer can be especially helpful in the estate planning process."

James E. Stiles, Certified Public Accountant

"After reading *The Artful Dodger's Guide to Planning Your Estate,* I now know how to explain to clients what I have been doing for years and I learned some new things as well."

Daniel I. Reith, Attorney at Law

"Heartiest congratulations! Terrific job of explaining sophisticated concepts in user-friendly language."

Henry Whiffen, Estate Planning Advisor

"In this concise guide written in plain English, Tom Hawley has produced a brief understandable explanation of a very complex subject."

James H. Flanagan, Jr., Esq., President,
American Benefit Development Corp.

"Important concepts made user friendly. A wonderful book."

Shary Farr, Life Planner, Hospice of the Central Coast

"There are some excellent books available that discuss trusts and estates. My favorite is The Artful Dodger's Guide to Planning Your Estate by Thomas Hart Hawley, of Carmel."

Ken Petersen in his weekly column, Financial Planning,
The Monterey Herald

"An elegantly simple and entertaining way to learn most of what we all should know about preparing for the future."

Dr. Richard Jobe, author of
The Sophisticated Shopper's Guide to Plastic Surgery

"For many years clients have asked me for books to read on estate planning. Most of the available tomes were too long, dry, and boring. Thomas Hawley has reversed the equation with a book that is short, accurate, and witty. I recommend it to all those interested in saving estate taxes."

William H. Bachrach, Attorney at Law

THE
ARTFUL DODGER'S
GUIDE TO PLANNING
YOUR ESTATE

THOMAS HART HAWLEY

Illustrated by Shell Fisher

THE ONLY BOOK ON ESTATE PLANNING
GUARANTEED TO KEEP YOU ENTERTAINED

Cover and Text Design: Irene Imfeld Graphic Design
Illustrations: Shell Fisher
Copy Editor: Diane H. Gibbs
Photographer: Steven A. Gann
Advisor: Jack Howell

Linthicum Press
P.O. Box 805
Carmel-by-the-Sea, CA 93921
Phone: (831) 624-5339
Fax: (831) 624-5839

ISBN 0-9649446-5-0

This publication is intended to provide accurate information about selected estate planning topics. It is not meant to be a substitute for working directly with a qualified attorney or other estate planning professional, but rather to help the reader prepare for such work.

This book is sold with the understanding that the author and the publisher are not engaged in rendering to the reader any legal, accounting, tax, or other professional services.

Every attempt has been made to assure the accuracy of the material here presented, but neither the author nor the publisher assumes liability for any error or omission.

Individual copies $17.95 plus $2.00 postage and handling. Discounts available for quantity orders. (See order form in back.)

Linthicum Press books are available at quantity discounts and customized editions to promote products or services. For information, please write Linthicum Press, P.O. Box 805, Carmel-by-the-Sea, CA 93921.

This book is dedicated to my parents,
to my own little Dodgers,
Inga and Kristina,
and to the memory of John Kaplan,
Professor of Law, Stanford University.

Contents

THE LIVING TRUST

OTHER IMPORTANT DOCUMENTS

CHILDREN

COMMUNITY PROPERTY

RETIREMENT PLANNING

LIFE INSURANCE

ASSET PROTECTION

CONSERVATORSHIPS

Preface

The first edition of this book sold well. This may be more a reflection of the size of my family than the merits of the book. Nonetheless, encouraged, I set about working on the second edition, which added the chapter "Halfway House for Big Givers" and corrected a few minor embarrassments.

Roughly ten minutes after the second edition had been printed, Uncle Sam announced the passage of the 1998 Taxpayer's Relief Act. The second edition was out of date before its ink had dried.

Undaunted, I set about writing the third edition, which I decided to change to a national edition. To this end, I deleted several chapters primarily of interest, if at all, to California residents; rewrote the others; and added six chapters dealing with retirement planning and living trusts.

This edition also has been updated to include the 1998 Taxpayer's Relief Act. I can only hope Uncle Sam will continue to be more interested in the moral peccadillos of our leaders than with tax reform so as to give this edition a chance.

Acknowledgements

I want to thank the following for their criticism (constant but, usually, constructive) of the first draft of this book: Jim Cook, Esq., Marijke Hartog, Charles Hawley, Kate Hawley, Melvin Hawley, Esq., Richard Henson, Esq., Michael L. McMahan, Esq., and W. R. Rosecrans, Esq.

I am especially grateful to Doug Thompson, Editor of *The Carmel Pine Cone,* for agreeing to take a chance on the column "Where There's a Will . . . ," and the many Carmel subscribers (well, actually two) who urged me to write this book.

Thanks also to the long-suffering efforts of my paralegal of 26 years, Carol Jarick, for her technical assistance and advice.

And to my running buddy, Shell Fisher, whose brilliant illustrations breathe life into the characters in this book.

I did my own word processing for this book. Every few minutes or so my computer screen would flash some message like "Error message number 23 reading floppy disk drive: 1. Retry 2. Cancel 3. Commit seppuku." Thank goodness for my friend and computer guru, Howard Nieman, who never complained about the late-night calls and always had a solution.

I wish to express my gratitude to Harold Boucher for his practical suggestions and the inspiration of his excellent book, *California Living Trusts and Wills* (Pennoyer Press, 1994).

Additionally, I wish to acknowledge the truly scrutinous efforts of the copy editor, Diane H. Gibbs, and the superb cover and text design by Irene Imfeld Graphic Design.

After this book was first published, a number of attorneys and other professionals provided very helpful comments on how it could be improved. My thanks to Yvonne A. Ascher, Esq., Thomas E. Mallett, Esq., Sidney M. Morris, Esq., John

Northcote, Esq., Jo Marie Ometer, Esq., James E. Stiles, C.P.A., Mark J. Welch, Esq., and Klar Wennerholm, Esq.

The most difficult chapters for me to write were the three on retirement planning (chapters 25–27). It took the efforts of Ute Isbill, Esq., and Kathleen Llewellyn, Esq., who provided the initial outline, to get me started, and the professional assistance of Michael J. Jones, C.P.A., the dean of retirement planners, who put the finishing touches on the chapters.

And finally, this book would not have happened without the unflagging efforts of Jack Howell of Morning Sun Press, who shepherded the project from first draft to final publication.

Introduction

Allow me to introduce The Artful Dodger. "Art," as he is known to his friends, is undergoing a midlife crisis. At Art's age this would not be unusual except that Art's crisis is different. While most men his age suddenly go out and spend gobs of money on a red Miata convertible, Art suddenly wants to *save* gobs of money, through estate planning.

He is aided by his "clever attorney," who not only gives Art sound advice but also, on occasion, keeps him from doing something really stupid.

In these pages you will also meet Ellie Dodger, Art's wife, along with the Dodgers' son, Roger, and Roger's kids, the six little Dodgers, along with sundry other Dodger relations.

The villain of the piece, of course, is Uncle Sam, who doggedly tries to deprive Art of his hard-earned booty.

The Dodgers will help illustrate the ways all of us can save both income and estate taxes through basic planning techniques.

This is not a "do-it-yourself" book. Quite the contrary. Estate planning is complex and best left to the experts. Instead, this book will give you the basics you need to better assist your own clever attorney in planning your estate. By knowing something about estate planning *before* consulting your attorney, you will save yourself both time and money.

Nor is this book about exotic tax loopholes that are fabulous if they work and disastrous if they don't. The techniques discussed here are well established and, if implemented by a professional, will not come back to disturb your sleep.

Within these pages you will not learn how to avoid paying your fair share of taxes. Rather, you will learn how to minimize the impact of taxes on you and your family by making use of strategies to which Uncle Sam himself, albeit grudgingly, has consented.

Finally, this book is an overview. It is not intended to make a lawyer out of you. Every tax rule has an exception and every exception has a qualification and so on. These complexities may be fascinating to lawyers, but to most folks, they are a bore. To encourage you to read past page 16, I have left out a lot of the tedious stuff.

One word of caution: Uncle Sam is a regular Prince Hamlet when it comes to making up his mind. He is always fiddling with the tax law. So be on guard for changes he may make after this book is published.

Much of the material in this book first appeared in a weekly newspaper column called "Where There's a Will . . . ." For this reason, the chapters are column length, which is helpful in allowing you to traverse estate planning one short step at a time.

So come join Art and his family in what I hope will be a worthwhile and even entertaining journey to this foreign land of QTIPs, QDOTs, and QPRTs. And if you pay close attention, you might just save enough in taxes to have that red Miata convertible.

"Big book, big bore."

Callimachus
(c. 305 – c. 240 B.C.)
Hellenistic Greek poet and critic known for his brevity

CHAPTER 1

Nuts and Bolts

The Artful Dodger has become obsessed lately with the idea of saving taxes. You can't blame Art. He comes by it honestly. For it was Art's grandfather Cornelius who, plagiarizing a famous philosopher, was fond of saying, "He, who does not understand taxes, is doomed to overpay them."

With the help of the Dodger clan, this little book explains in simple terms planning techniques that can save you and your family from the often devastating effect of death taxes. You cannot understand these techniques without knowing a little about our federal estate and gift tax structure. Therefore, the first two chapters will provide you with an overview of this structure.

To spare you a good deal of mind-numbing verbiage, what follows has been kept to a simple nuts-and-bolts description.

ESTATE AND GIFT TAXES

Uncle Sam taxes gifts you make during your life and at death. In medieval times (i.e., before 1977) lifetime gifts were taxed at a different rate from gifts made at death. Today the same tax rates apply to all gifts, whether they are made during life or at death.

THE LIFETIME EXEMPTION

The good news is that each of you has a lifetime exemption equal to $650,000 in 1999, $675,000 in 2000 and 2001. This exemption gradually increases until 2006 when it will top out at

$1,000,000. Although this increase is not to be sneezed at, it averages only about 6% per year—barely enough to keep up with inflation. In the interests of simplicity, I will use $650,000 as the exemption amount in this book, although you and I know it is a moving target. This lifetime exemption allows you to transfer during your lifetime or at death $650,000 free of any gift or estate tax. Let's see how this exemption works.

Let's assume, hypothetically, that Grandfather Cornelius died leaving his $1,000,000 estate to his favorite grandson, Art. (Unfortunately, this is purely hypothetical since Grandfather C actually left all his loot to a 26-year-old aroma therapist; but that's another story.) The first $650,000 would pass free of tax. Art would pay a whopping $134,600 on the remaining $350,000, however, because the bad news is that tax rates start out high.

The first dollar over $650,000 is taxed at 37%. Rates gradually increase until they reach 55% on estates exceeding $3,000,000. Finally, in estates valued at over $10,000,000, the $650,000 exemption, like the Cheshire cat's smile, begins to disappear, until at $17,184,000, it is gone altogether.

ANNUAL EXCLUSION GIFTS

Uncle Sam also allows you to give $10,000 each year to each of any number of people tax free. (Beginning in 1998, the amount of the annual exclusion adjusts upwards for inflation in $1,000 increments.) This annual exclusion offers dramatic tax-saving opportunities. For example, Art has one child, Roger, and six grandchildren, the little Dodgers. Art can give $10,000 to each of these family members and instantly reduce his taxable estate by $70,000. In fact, if Art makes the gift on the evening of December 31, he can make another gift, as soon as his head has cleared, the next morning and remove $140,000 from his estate!

Uncle Sam used to disallow any gifts made within three years of death. But no more. Now even a deathbed gift works.

THE UNLIMITED
MARITAL DEDUCTION

Since 1981, transfers between spouses during lifetime or at death are not taxed. The transfers must be outright (or in other qualifying forms, which we will get into later).

In theory, Art could leave his entire estate to his wife, Ellie Dodger, who could then leave the estate to her new, presumably younger, husband, who could later leave the estate to his new, presumably younger, wife, and so on. In this way, theoretically, fortunes could pass down through the ages untaxed. In reality, most of us cannot get too excited about estate plans calculated to save taxes for our posthumous marital replacements.

Now let's take a look at how death taxes are computed. Then we will roll up our sleeves and begin looking at various ways of avoiding these taxes.

More Nuts and Bolts

Let's see just how Uncle Sam goes about taxing your property at your death.

The Artful Dodger, when feeling expansive, often gestures toward his home, Chez Dodger, and declares proudly to his son, Roger Dodger, "Someday, all of this will belong to you!" This is unfortunate not only because it is a cliché but also because it is not quite true. Though lacking in dramatic effect, it would be more literal for Art to say, "Someday, all of this will belong to you . . . and your partner, Uncle Sam."

For indeed, Uncle Sam is a silent partner who lays claim to his share of your property at death. In computing that share the first step is to determine the value of your gross estate.

YOUR GROSS ESTATE

Your house, your yacht, your Nordic Track, all property you own at death is included in your gross estate.

Uncle Sam, in a rare sporting gesture, allows your representative to value your property at either the date of your death or six months later. It's a no-lose proposition since the election can be made after the six months have passed, when the values on both dates are known. For example, let's say Grandfather Cornelius's entire estate consisted of stock in Excelsior, Inc. worth $1,000,000 at his death, which declined in value to $700,000 six months later. Grandfather C's representative will choose to have the estate valued six months after Grandfather C's death at $700,000, thus saving tax on the $300,000 difference!

It is a common misconception that life insurance is not taxable at death. If Art owns a $100,000 policy of insurance on his life, naming his son, Roger, as the beneficiary, the $100,000 will be taxable in his estate at death. If, on the other hand, Roger owns the same policy on Art's life, none of the proceeds will be taxable on Art's death and Roger will receive the $100,000 tax free.

Joint tenancy assets are included in your gross estate unless the other joint tenant contributed to the cost of the asset. For example, if Art owns a home in joint tenancy with Roger, unless Roger contributed to the cost of the home, its entire value will be included in Art's estate.

The rule is different if Art holds property in joint tenancy with his wife, Ellie. Then, only half of the property is included in his gross estate regardless of who paid for the asset. The same is true of assets held with Ellie as community property.

YOUR TAXABLE ESTATE

Your taxable estate is computed by subtracting from your gross estate, certain deductions such as funeral expenses, administration expenses, and debts (your home mortgage, for example). Gifts to your spouse and to charity are also subtracted.

A "tentative" tax is then computed on your taxable estate. It is tentative because it is reduced by $211,300 (which is the tax on the $650,000 that you can transfer tax free). The effect of these machinations is to exempt from tax the first $650,000 of your taxable estate.

INHERITANCE TAX

No need to fret, at least for most of you. In roughly two-thirds of the states (see Appendix A), there isn't any. These states do impose a "pickup" tax, however. Once your estate tax is computed, a portion of it is sent to your state treasurer and the balance to Uncle Sam. This sharing of revenue has no effect on the total estate tax. So it doesn't cost you anything.

The remaining states have their own varieties of estate and inheritance taxes, which, if you live there, you will just have to look up.

So much for the bird's-eye view. Now let's have a look at some of the details from the worm's vantage point and get on with the business of saving taxes.

CHAPTER 3

Uncle Sam's Worst Nightmare

One of the goals of the Artful Dodger, of course, is to provide for his wife, Ellie, at his death. Uncle Sam assists this goal by allowing Art to make tax-free gifts of any size to Ellie during life or at death. This is known as the unlimited marital deduction.

Art must keep one important limitation in mind, however. The gift to Ellie must be outright, that is, without strings attached. For example, even if Art has visions of Ellie lavishing his hard-earned money on her new husband, he can't make a gift to her that will end on her remarriage.

This requirement of an outright gift once created problems for many taxpayers. For example, take the case of Art's son, Roger Dodger. Roger is married to Thelma, by whom he has six children, the little Dodgers. Thelma also has children by a prior marriage. Roger wants to leave his estate to Thelma for her use during her life. At Thelma's death, however, Roger wants what's left to pass to his kids, the six little Dodgers, not to hers.

Roger's in a bind. If he leaves his property to Thelma, outright, Thelma might just bequeath Roger's estate to her own children or, God forbid, to her new husband. If, on the other hand, Roger leaves his property to her in trust, the gift is not outright and does not qualify for the unlimited marital deduction. Consequently, at Roger's death, Thelma will pay estate tax on everything over $650,000.

THE QTIP TRUST

In an attempt to solve this problem, Uncle Sam, in 1981, created the QTIP trust. (Believe me, you don't want to know what

QTIP stands for. But if you insist, it stands for "qualified terminable interest property"). Now Roger can leave his property to a QTIP trust for the benefit of Thelma and have it qualify for the marital deduction. Thelma must have the right to receive all trust income and to require the trustee to invest in assets that produce a reasonable return. Roger can also give Thelma the right to receive support from the trust. In fact, Roger can name Thelma to act as her own trustee.

On Thelma's death, however, Roger can direct that what's left of his estate will pass to his children. The assets of the QTIP trust will be included in Thelma's estate for estate tax purposes. But any tax generated by the QTIP trust will be paid by the little Dodgers, not by Thelma's beneficiaries.

THE QUALIFIED DOMESTIC TRUST

After Uncle Sam gave us the unlimited marital deduction, he started having recurring nightmares. He dreamed of the millionaire who dies leaving all of his money, tax free, to his wife, who happens to be a citizen of Raritania. The bereaved widow takes her entire inheritance back to her native Raritania. On her death it is the King of Raritania, not Uncle Sam, who collects death taxes. (At this point Uncle Sam would wake up sweaty and nearly hysterical.)

Uncle Sam created the qualified domestic trust (or QDOT) to ensure that gifts to noncitizens stayed in the United States where they eventually could be taxed. If either you or your spouse is not a U.S. citizen, you must pay close attention to what follows. Otherwise you can now skip directly to the next chapter.

Even if your spouse is not a citizen, if you leave him or her $650,000 or less, it doesn't matter, since your gift will be protected by your lifetime exemption. If you leave your spouse more, the excess will not qualify for the marital deduction, and hence will be subject to tax, unless it passes to a qualified domestic trust. The most significant features of this trust are that one of the trustees must be a U.S. citizen and estate taxes must be withheld if distributions of trust principal are made to your spouse. (Distributions of trust income, however, are not subject to estate tax.)

On your spouse's death, since the qualified domestic trust is in the United States rather than, for example, Raritania, Uncle Sam finally gets to collect the estate tax. As in the case of the QTIP trust, the assets of the qualified domestic trust are included in your spouse's taxable estate. Estate taxes generated by the assets are paid by the qualified domestic trust, however, not by your spouse's beneficiaries.

Did you know that many married couples waste one of their lifetime exemptions? If you do not want the dubious distinction of being a member of this class, read on.

4

Getting Two Exemptions
for the Price of One

Estate planning would be a simple matter if all the Artful Dodger had to do was write a will leaving his property to his wife, Ellie. If the gift to Ellie was outright or to a QTIP trust, Ellie would pay no estate taxes on Art's death. But Art might be creating problems down the road.

Let's assume Art leaves $1,000,000 to Ellie. At Art's death, due to the unlimited marital deduction, this gift will pass to Ellie tax free. So far so good. Now assume Ellie bequeaths $1,400,000 (consisting of the money Art left her plus $400,000 of her own money) to the Dodgers' child, Roger.

Here's the rub. The bequest to Roger is not protected by the unlimited marital deduction. It is, therefore, taxable. After deducting Ellie's $650,000 exemption, Roger will pay estate tax on the remaining $750,000 in the amount of $301,500.

Somehow Art's $650,000 exemption got lost in the shuffle. Is there any way to avoid this nasty result? Yes, and here's how.

THE BYPASS TRUST

This time let's assume that instead of leaving the entire $1,000,000 to Ellie, outright, Art places $650,000 in a bypass trust. (It is called a bypass trust because on Ellie's death the property bypasses being taxed in her estate.) This $650,000 does not qualify for the marital deduction, but it is protected by Art's lifetime exemption and so passes to Ellie free of tax.

Now, at Ellie's death $650,000 of her estate is not taxed, because it is protected by her lifetime exemption. And the $650,000 Art put in the bypass trust is not taxed either, because since Ellie didn't own it, it is not part of her estate. Roger will pay tax on only the remaining $100,000 in the amount of $37,000—a tax saving of $264,500.

Of course, Art is suspicious. "How will this bypass trust limit Ellie's enjoyment of the property?" he asks. As it turns out, not much.

Art can give Ellie one or more of these rights and still keep the property out of her estate:

(1) The right to receive all the income from the trust.
(2) The right to receive from the trust whatever amounts are necessary for her reasonable support.
(3) The right to take out 5% of the value of the trust each year with no questions asked.
(4) The right to choose which children or grandchildren will inherit the property at Ellie's death.

Art can even avoid trustee's fees by naming Ellie as her own trustee.

You think I'm not aware that your eyes are starting to glaze over? This is the toughest stuff you will have to learn, so don't be discouraged. To help you through this labyrinth, I have prepared two charts (Appendix B) to show you just how all this fits together.

BALANCING THE ESTATES

When one spouse has more assets than the other, it is possible to lose part of the combined $1,300,000 exemption of both spouses. Let me explain. Assume Art has separate property worth $1,300,000 and Ellie has nothing. If Art dies first, no problem (at least from the standpoint of saving taxes). Art can

---

put $650,000 in the bypass trust and give $650,000 outright or in a QTIP trust to Ellie. At Ellie's death both the bypass trust and what's left in Ellie's estate (up to the amount of her exemption) will pass to Roger tax free.

But if Ellie dies first, since she has no assets her $650,000 lifetime exemption will be wasted. At Art's death, Roger will pay tax on the remaining $650,000 in Art's estate that is not protected by Art's exemption.

One solution is for Art to make a lifetime gift to Ellie of $650,000, thereby balancing both estates. Then no matter who dies first, neither spouse's exemption will be wasted. Needless to say, prior to making any gifts to Ellie, Art should obtain independent legal advice because the gift to Ellie is irrevocable.

OVERFUNDING THE BYPASS TRUST

Now I am going to make a really shocking suggestion. What if at Art's death Art's representative (who is probably Ellie) put $750,000 instead of $650,000 in the bypass trust? Art's exemption will protect only $650,000. True, on Art's death Ellie will pay tax on the extra $100,000. But the tax will be at the lowest estate tax rate (37%). And at Ellie's death that $100,000 (less $37,000 of estate taxes paid at Art's death) plus any appreciation will not be taxed in her estate at higher rates.

In larger estates, your spouse can actually choose to have property taxed upon your death at 37% instead of 55% at your spouse's death. In theory this is an excellent way to save taxes. In practice, however, most of us are not too keen on the idea of incurring a tax now, even at lower rates, that can be delayed until our death.

Now it's time for a real-life case history to see how the QTIP and the bypass trusts work hand in hand to save taxes. So don't click, stay right here.

Putting It All Together

Federal law requires the following consumer protection warning: "It has been determined that this chapter is uncommonly tiresome. Do not read this chapter while operating a motor vehicle."

THE TWO-TRUST PLAN

Let's see how the QTIP and bypass trusts can be used in setting up a tax-efficient estate plan for Art and Ellie. Art's will might read something like this:

> I confirm to my wife, Ellie, her one-half of our community property and all her separate property. By this will I intend to dispose of my one-half of the community property and all my separate property.
>
> At my death my executor shall divide my estate into two trusts called the Art Dodger bypass trust and the Art Dodger QTIP trust. My executor shall put assets equal in value to my lifetime exemption [for example, in the year 1999, $650,000] into my bypass trust and the rest of my assets into my QTIP trust [or if Ellie is not a U.S. citizen, my qualified domestic trust].
>
> I appoint Ellie as the trustee of these trusts, but if she cannot serve, I appoint my son, Roger, as the successor trustee.
>
> The trustee shall pay Ellie all the income from my QTIP trust at least annually and as much of the principal as is necessary for her support in accordance with her

accustomed manner of living. If Ellie disclaims [see chapter 8] any part of the QTIP trust, that part shall be added to the bypass trust.

The trustee shall also pay Ellie as much of the income or principal of the bypass trust as is necessary for her support in accordance with her accustomed standard of living. However, the trustee can make these payments only after taking into consideration any other assets (including Ellie's own property and the assets in my QTIP trust) available to Ellie for her support.

At Ellie's death my QTIP and bypass trusts shall be distributed to my son, Roger, if he survives Ellie, and if he does not, to my grandchildren, the little Dodgers, in equal shares.

CAUTION

As a concession to the attention span of my readers, I have oversimplified this will. It should *not* be used by Art, Ellie, or any of you. You can anticipate that the Dodger's Clever Attorney (or yours) will take this simple document and, through the miracle of word processing, transform it instantly into 27 pages of legal prose that will make heavy the eyelids of the most chronic insomniac.

ADVANTAGES

To summarize, this estate plan accomplishes several important goals:

- Art's lifetime exemption is preserved in the bypass trust so that at Ellie's death, the bypass trust passes to Roger tax free.
- The QTIP trust (or the qualified domestic trust if Ellie is not a U.S. citizen) qualifies for the unlimited marital deduction and so is not taxable at Art's death.

- Art's will controls to whom both his trusts are distributed at Ellie's death.
- Requiring the trustee to distribute the bypass trust to Ellie *only* after taking into account Ellie's other resources, including the QTIP trust, saves taxes at Ellie's death, for it forces Ellie to consume the QTIP trust first (which will be taxable in her estate) and the bypass trust last (which will pass tax free to Roger).
- Giving Ellie the option to disclaim the QTIP trust assets into the bypass trust allows Ellie to "overfund" the bypass trust. She can thus choose to incur a tax at Art's death at tax rates lower than at her death.
- Neither trust will be subject to probate at Ellie's death, and if properly drafted neither trust will be subject to the claims of Ellie's creditors.

So, as you can see, these trusts are pretty hot stuff. But Ellie must pay careful attention to what she is doing as trustee of these trusts, or she could end up in some pretty hot water.

The Trustee Trap

Like the ghost of Christmas future, let me transport you to a time 20 years hence. Art has died, and Ellie now finds herself as the trustee of these wonderful tax-saving trusts we've been talking about. Fortunately, the Clever Attorney, although more long-winded and suffering from a bit of short-term memory loss, still can be relied on for sound advice.

Thank goodness, because too often attorneys fail to warn surviving spouses of some dangerous pitfalls that await the unsuspecting trustee. These pitfalls are more perilous (1) in situations where the ultimate beneficiaries of the trust are not the children of the trustee or (2) in cases of family discord. To give this narrative some much needed dramatic tension, we will assume that Ellie and Roger are not on friendly terms. Therefore, the Clever Attorney advises Ellie that she must toe the line.

FIDUCIARY DUTY

As trustee, Ellie has a fiduciary (derived from the Latin "fido," meaning loyal cartoon dog) duty toward Roger and the little Dodgers, who are the ultimate beneficiaries of the trusts. This is the highest duty imposed by the law, so Ellie must take this responsibility seriously. This duty includes . . .

THE DUTY OF IMPARTIALITY

Ellie cannot favor one beneficiary (i.e., herself) over another (i.e., Roger). For example, assuming Ellie has no assets of her own, how much can she pay herself from Art's trusts for her support? Can she take a cruise? If so, can she travel first class or must she go steerage? Can she eat caviar or must she eat rattrap cheese? No matter how much or how little Ellie takes out of Art's trusts, Roger no doubt will consider it excessive, for every penny Ellie takes out is a penny less that Roger will eventually receive.

THE DUTY
TO ACCOUNT

Ellie must provide Roger and the little Dodgers with periodic accountings detailing such things as income, expenses, gains and losses on sales of assets, etc. This requires basic accounting skills and a knowledge of the Principal and Income Act. Ellie must also file income tax returns for Art's trusts. In short, Ellie had better retain the services of a Clever Accountant to help her in these complex matters.

THE DUTY
NOT TO SELF-DEAL

Ellie must take special care in situations in which her personal interests may be (or may appear to be) in conflict with those of the trusts. Let's say one of Art's trusts owns one-half of the Dodgers' residence and Ellie owns the other. Ellie wants to buy out the trust's one-half so she can own 100% of the residence. Even if Ellie pays a fair price for the home, Roger can void the transaction on the basis that Ellie as trustee violated her fiduciary duty by dealing with herself.

THE DUTY TO MAKE PROPERTY
PRODUCTIVE

As trustee Ellie has the duty to invest trust assets prudently. Many states have passed laws setting out investment standards that trustees must follow. For example, in most states Ellie has a duty to diversify trust investments. She must also protect Roger's interests from inflationary devaluation by investing for growth as well as income. Unless Ellie is an expert herself, she should seek investment assistance from a professional.

THE DUTY TO KEEP TRUSTS SEPARATE

Art's bypass trust will pass to Roger tax free, but Art's QTIP trust will be taxable in Ellie's estate. Therefore, Ellie must keep the two trusts separate, that is, separate accounts, separate tax identification numbers, and separate tax returns. For if she doesn't, Uncle Sam will tax the bypass trust in Ellie's estate and less will pass to Roger (which, in view of Roger's shabby behavior, may not be such a bad result).

HOW TO MAKE IT BETTER

Obviously, the last thing Art intended was that his inspired estate plan would result in Ellie and Roger at each other's throats. Art could have prevented some problems by stating his intentions more specifically in his will. For example, if he wanted Ellie to have more flexibility in making distributions of support to herself, he could have stated that his primary objective was the welfare of Ellie and that "support" should be liberally construed in her favor. Or if Art felt that no words would be sufficient to prevent internecine bloodshed, he could have named a bank as trustee rather than Ellie. Corporate trustees, although they charge roughly 1% of the value of the trust annually, can be invaluable in preserving harmonious family relationships (or, at the very least, preventing murder).

Finally, Ellie can sidestep most of the pitfalls by seeking the assistance of the court. For example, before Ellie purchases the residence from Art's trust, she can file a petition seeking court approval. At the hearing, the judge will make an order after considering the positions of all beneficiaries. If the court decides in Ellie's favor, she can purchase the residence without fearing a sniper attack from Roger.

Time to wake up back in the present and take a look at an often overlooked way to save your grandchildren lots of taxes.

Passing Wealth Tax Free to Your Grandchildren

Before we go any further, I must lay to rest a persistent rumor. This book is not about to be made into a major motion picture starring Clint Eastwood as the unlimited marital deduction. Now that we've scotched this bit of gossip, let's get back to the business of saving taxes.

The planning techniques we've discussed so far have been aimed at saving your spouse and your children taxes. Some of you may want to take the longer view and look at ways to save your grandchildren taxes as well.

TAXING EACH GENERATION

Let's again turn to our favorite taxpayers to help illustrate. The Dodgers' son, Roger, as we know, has six children. Roger has made a fortune speculating in pork bellies. When the Dodgers leave their money to Roger, it will be taxed in the estate of either Art or Ellie, whoever dies last. Since Roger is already wealthy, he may not spend his inheritance. Therefore, at Roger's death what's left of his parents' money will be taxed again in his estate before passing to his children.

It occurs to Art, who though avaricious is not so dumb, that this double estate tax could be avoided if he gave his money directly to his grandchildren (Roger's children). In this way Art's money would not be taxed in Roger's estate but would pass directly to the little Dodgers.

For many years Art's idea worked. Taxpayers gave as much money as they wanted to their grandchildren so the money would escape being taxed in the estates of their children. Gifts of this type came to be known as generation-skipping transfers.

Uncle Sam finally said "enough is enough" and in 1976 made his first attempt to limit generation-skipping transfers.

THE $1,000,000 GRANDCHILD'S EXEMPTION

Today, each of us has a $1,000,000 "grandchild's exemption." (In truth, this sobriquet is a tad misleading. This exemption applies to transfers not only to Art's grandchildren but also to any other beneficiaries more than one generation younger than Art. Also, commencing 1998 this exemption increases by inflation in $10,000 increments. But we'll keep referring to it as "the $1,000,000 grandchild's exemption" to keep things simple.)

This means, for example, that Art can leave $1,000,000 to his grandchildren. Just like in the good old days this $1,000,000 will not be taxed in Roger's estate. But now Uncle Sam taxes gifts in excess of $1,000,000 to grandchildren with a vengeance. Not only will Art's estate be taxed on the amount of any gift to the little Dodgers in excess of $1,000,000, but Uncle Sam also adds on a rapacious generation-skipping penalty, which is due nine months after Art's death.

The trick is to limit generation-skipping transfers to $1,000,000 and not a penny more. So Art and Ellie must content themselves with each giving no more than $1,000,000 ($2,000,000 in all) to their grandchildren.

THE GENERATION-SKIPPING TRUST

Since money won speculating in pork bellies can be lost speculating in pork bellies, Ellie is worried that Roger may need the $1,000,000 after all. No problem. Instead of leaving $1,000,000 outright to her grandchildren, Ellie can leave the money, in trust, to Roger for Roger's life, with the balance passing to the little Dodgers at Roger's death. Roger can even be his own trustee.

If Roger needs the money, he can withdraw what he reasonably requires for his living expenses. Or Roger can leave the money in the trust and watch it grow. Of course, the income earned by the trust is taxed each year. But at Roger's death whatever is left in the trust will pass to the little Dodgers without being taxed in Roger's estate—hence the name, generation-skipping trust.

The potential tax savings are pretty heady stuff. Let's assume Roger survives his mother by 20 years and that money invested wisely doubles every ten years. At Roger's death Ellie's $1,000,000 will have increased to $4,000,000, and the entire $4,000,000 will pass to the little Dodgers without being taxed in Roger's estate.

Art can do the same thing, which will pass twice as much, tax free, to the little Dodgers. In fact, Art and Ellie can first each leave the $1,000,000 to the other in trust. Only at the death of the survivor will the $2,000,000 pass into Roger's trust.

To illustrate this technique (and because I have recently become quite good at making boxes and lines on my word processor), I have prepared a chart for you (Appendix C).

BALANCING THE ESTATES

Remember in chapter 4 how a gift from Art to Ellie avoided wasting Ellie's $650,000 exemption? Good! Because the same technique applies to generation-skipping transfers.

Assume Art has separate property worth over $2,000,000 and Ellie has nothing. If Art dies first, he can leave his estate to Ellie in such a way that both he and Ellie can make full use of Art's $1,000,000 grandchild's exemption, and a total of $2,000,000 (plus appreciation) will pass to the little Dodgers without being taxed in Roger's estate.

But if Ellie dies first, her exemption will be lost and only $1,000,000 (plus appreciation) can pass to the little Dodgers tax free. After consulting independent legal counsel, Art may decide to make a lifetime gift to Ellie of $1,000,000, thereby assuring that both exemptions will be protected regardless of who dies first.

Although generation-skipping transfers provide dramatic tax savings, most taxpayers overlook this valuable planning tool.

In the next chapter, Art's ship finally comes in. But, alas, too late.

Thanks, But No Thanks

Last week the Artful Dodger's ship finally came in. Art's Aunt Agatha died at the age of 92 and left him a tidy sum. Years ago this would have been cause for celebration (after Art had worked through his grief, of course). But now, Art doesn't need the money. The inheritance will only increase the size of Art's estate and push him into a higher estate tax bracket.

TOO MUCH, TOO LATE

Fortunately, Art has never been one to hold things in. And one evening at the local watering hole, Mac's Tea Room, Art complained to his Clever Attorney about his ship that came too late. Art's Clever Attorney suggested that Art drop in the next morning with a copy of Aunt Agatha's will to see if anything could be done.

Aunt Agatha's will contained the following gift to Art: "To my tightwad nephew, Artful Dodger, I give the sum of $100,000, if he survives me, and if he does not, I give this sum to his son, Roger."

THE SOLUTION

Art's Clever Attorney explained that the solution to Art's problem was for Art to disclaim the $100,000 gift. A disclaimer is a legal way of saying "Thanks, but no thanks." If Art disclaims the gift, the $100,000 will pass to Roger as if Art had died before his aunt. This is a once-in-a-lifetime opportunity for Art to make a tax-free gift to Roger without using up any of his lifetime exemption.

THE TECHNICAL STUFF

Not surprisingly, however, Uncle Sam has established some strict requirements for disclaimers:

(1) Art's disclaimer must be in writing.
(2) Art must make the disclaimer within nine months of Aunt Agatha's death.
(3) Art cannot receive any benefits from the gift. For example, if Art had received the interest from the $100,000, he would be out of luck.
(4) Art cannot direct where the gift goes. But Aunt Agatha can. She has named Art's son, Roger, to receive the $100,000 if Art dies before her. Therefore, the gift will pass to Roger, if Art disclaims, without any direction from Art.
(5) The disclaimer must be irrevocable. Once the disclaimer is filed with the probate court,

> *Nor all your piety,*
> *nor wit shall lure it back*
> *to cancel half a line;*
> *nor all your tears*
> *wash out a word of it.*

So Art must reflect seriously on what he is about to do.

Art, upon reflection, decides it would be nice, after all, to have, say, $25,000 to take his wife, Ellie, on a long-promised cruise. No problem. Art can disclaim only $75,000 and keep the balance.

A WORD OF CAUTION

However, there is a flaw in the ointment (as Mrs. Malaprop would say). Remember the generation-skipping tax we talked about in the last chapter? Of course you do! Well, if Art makes a disclaimer, it's as if the gift passed directly from Aunt Agatha to Roger. Since Roger is more than one generation below Aunt Agatha, the gift could be subject to the confiscatory generation-skipping tax if Aunt Agatha has already used up her $1,000,000 grandchild's exemption. Before making the disclaimer, Art should talk to Aunt Agatha's attorney to make sure he is not walking into a tax trap.

OTHER USES
OF DISCLAIMERS

As we will see in future chapters, disclaimers can also be used to reassign benefits payable from insurance policies, annuities, or retirement accounts. For example, Art can name Ellie as the primary beneficiary of his life insurance with his bypass trust as the first contingent beneficiary and Roger as the second contingent beneficiary. If, at Art's death, Art's estate is not large enough to fully fund the bypass trust, Ellie can disclaim her rights as beneficiary and the insurance proceeds will flow into the bypass trust to the extent needed to top it off to $650,000. If, on the other hand, neither Ellie nor the bypass trust needs the proceeds, Ellie can disclaim her rights both as the primary beneficiary and as trustee of the bypass trust and the proceeds will pass to Roger.

Next we'll look at one of the simplest tax-saving devices that over time can yield huge rewards.

The Mouse That Roared

Most of you probably know that every year you can give away $10,000 to each of any number of people tax free. (Commencing in 1998, this $10,000 increases for inflation in $1,000 increments.) What you may not fully appreciate is the magnitude of the tax savings that can be achieved by this simple device. This so-called annual exclusion is truly the mouse that roared.

For example, take our friend, the Artful Dodger. Art can give $10,000 to his son, Roger, and each of the six little Dodgers ($70,000 in all) each calendar year tax free. If Art's wife, Ellie, joins in the gift, together they can give $140,000.

In just a few years Art and Ellie can give away substantial sums of money that would otherwise be taxed at their deaths.

There is one important restriction. The gifts must be of a present interest to qualify for the annual exclusion. In other words, the gifts must have no strings attached. Art will be quick to point out that one of his grandchildren is only 14. He is understandably reluctant to give $10,000 to a teenager who is likely to turn around and "invest" the money in the most expensive dirt bike in the county.

THE MINOR'S TRUST

Uncle Sam, who, for all we know, may have grandchildren of his own, has tried to solve Art's problem by creating what's known as the minor's trust. Art can give $10,000 each year to a trust for the benefit of each minor grandchild, and the gift will qualify for the $10,000 annual exclusion. Uncle Sam insists that the trust money be available for the benefit of the child until he or she reaches age 21, at which time the money must be payable to the child upon demand. Moreover, if the child dies before reaching age 21, the money is included in the minor's estate.

THE UNIFORM TRANSFERS
TO MINORS ACT

Uncle Sam also allows for tax-free gifts to minors under the Uniform Transfers to Minors Act, which most states have adopted. As in the case of the minor's trust, the money must be paid to the child at age 21 (age 25, if the gift is made at Art's death). The advantage of this type of gift is that it usually can be accomplished without the benefit of high-priced legal talent.

A CRUMMEY TRUST.

In a famous tax case a taxpayer by the name of Mr. Crummey (no kidding, that's his real name) was not satisfied with either of these two options. He was horrified at the thought of his children getting their hands on the trust money at age 21. So Mr. Crummey and his Clever Attorney drafted a different kind of trust.

It provided that when Mr. Crummey transferred $10,000 to a child's trust, the child had the right to take the $10,000 out the same year, thus satisfying the requirement that the gift be of a present interest. If the child didn't, the money would remain in the trust until the child was 35. (Mr. Crummey could have chosen any age.) Mr. Crummey never intended that a child exercise his or her right of withdrawal. And since Mr. Crummey could disinherit any child who did, it's a good bet that Mr. Crummey got his way.

Mr. Crummey's trust has been upheld by the courts and is now a popular estate-planning device. You can hardly blame attorneys for preferring the minor's trust, however. For it can hardly be good for business to have a client running around town telling all his friends that his attorney drafted a "Crummey trust."

THE "EMPOWERED" CRUMMEY

For over 20 years Mr. Crummey hogged the legal limelight as the popularity of his trust increased. Then along came Ms. Cristofani. She wanted to make annual exclusion gifts to her children and grandchildren *but* she wanted her children to have the enjoyment of the entire trust property during their lifetimes, with the trust passing to the grandchildren only on the death of her children. So Ms. Cristofani had her Clever Attorney draft a trust that did just that.

Uncle Sam, who liked the Crummey trust not a dime's worth, went fruitcake over this "empowered" Crummey. And no wonder, for it gives taxpayers such as the Dodgers a new way to save taxes.

For example, each year Art and Ellie can give $140,000 to Roger and the six little Dodgers in trust. Roger and each of the little Dodgers must be given the right to withdraw $20,000 during the year of the gift. And, voila, a perfect trust every time! For it achieves the following:

(1) The gift is tax free;
(2) Roger is the lifetime beneficiary of the *entire* trust;
(3) On Roger's death, the property passes to the little Dodgers free of any tax in Roger's estate; and
(4) None of Art's or Ellie's $1,000,000 grandchild's exemption is used up.

Uncle Sam's continuing fulminations so far have been in vain, and the Cristofani trust is gaining acceptance as a valuable planning tool.

In the next chapter we will look at gifts of different sizes, at least one of which is guaranteed to fit.

Gifts in Three
Different Sizes

Making gifts, especially to family members, is one of the most effective ways to save estate taxes. Since the Artful Dodger's path to earthly bliss is through tax avoidance, he is anxious to learn all he can about gifts, which, as it turns out, come in three convenient sizes—small, medium, and large.

ANNUAL
EXCLUSION GIFTS

As you know, each calendar year Art can give $10,000 to his son, Roger, and to each of Roger's six children tax free (or to anyone else, for that matter). Art and his wife, Ellie, together can give twice this amount. What you may not know is that Art can also pay the medical expenses and tuition of Roger and his children. For these gifts to be tax free, however, Art must pay the money directly to the medical care provider or the educational institution.

But what if Art becomes incompetent and loses the capacity to make a gift? On the advice of his Clever Attorney, Art has executed a Durable General Power of Attorney (see chapter 22) giving his agent the power to make annual exclusion gifts to family members. If Art becomes incompetent, his trustee (probably Ellie) can continue to pay $10,000 each year to the little Dodgers on Art's behalf.

GIFTS PROTECTED BY THE EXEMPTION

Like every other taxpayer, Art was born with a bellybutton and a lifetime exemption. This means Art can give away during his life or at his death a total of $650,000 (increasing to $1,000,000 by 2006) tax free. Art used to view this exemption much as a squirrel views nuts stored for the winter. The last thing he wanted to do was to consume it. After a chat with his Clever Attorney, however, Art had a change of heart.

For example, Art owns a summer cabin worth $150,000. If Art gives the cabin to Roger, he will use up $150,000 of his exemption, true. But the cabin plus any increase in its value will be removed from Art's estate. If the cabin appreciates $100,000 between the date of the gift and the date of Art's death, estate taxes on this $100,000 will have been saved.

GIFTS IN EXCESS OF THE EXEMPTION

Art was so impressed with his Clever Attorney's advice that he used up his entire $650,000 exemption by making gifts to Roger and the little Dodgers. Believe it or not, from now on, Art can make additional gifts at a bargain price. Let me explain.

To make it simple, let's assume Art is in a 50% estate and gift tax bracket. If Art now gives Roger $100,000, he will have to pay a gift tax of $50,000. It will, therefore, cost Art $150,000 to make a $100,000 gift. If Art doesn't make the gift but, instead, bequeaths Roger $150,000 in his will, at Art's death his estate will pay a tax of $75,000 on that $150,000. In other words, it will cost $150,000 to make a $75,000 gift.

How can this be? I told you earlier that tax rates for gifts and estates are the same. This is the truth, but it's not the whole truth. Uncle Sam doesn't tax the tax on gifts. But he does tax the tax on estates. As a result, it is one-third cheaper to give your estate away during your life than at death.

BE CAREFUL!

Art must take something very important into account before making a gift. Let's look again at Art's summer cabin, for which he paid $10,000 many years ago. (We call this $10,000 Art's tax basis.) If Art gives the summer cabin to Roger, Roger will take over Art's $10,000 tax basis. If Roger sells the cabin, he will pay capital gains tax on everything he receives over $10,000.

If, on the other hand, Art bequeaths the cabin to Roger, Roger will receive a new tax basis equal to the value of the cabin at Art's death, say $250,000. If Roger sells the cabin for $250,000, he will pay no capital gains tax.

The solution is for Art to give Roger assets that have not appreciated (such as cash, bonds, or his Costco stock) or assets that Roger is not likely to sell during his lifetime (such as the summer cabin). Likewise, Art should hold onto assets that have gone up in value.

As a final caution, before making any large gifts to Roger, Art should dust off Shakespeare's Collected Works and reread *King Lear*.

As a lad, Uncle Sam napped through Euclidian geometry. We'll see next just how this can work to your advantage.

CHAPTER 11

Non-Euclidian Gifts

Uncle Sam has some rather embarrassing gaps in his formal education, geometry being one. (In fact, if the truth be known, Uncle Sam thinks Euclid refers to a tribe of North American Eskimos.) Therefore, he never grasped the basic Euclidian hypothesis that the whole is equal to the sum of its parts. Uncle Sam's loss can be your gain, especially when it comes to making annual exclusion gifts of large assets, such as the family business or a vacation home, to younger generations. Allow me to explain.

Let's assume Art and Ellie own a business that has recently been appraised at $200,000. The Dodgers want to transfer the business to Roger so it will not be taxed in their estate. As I hope you know by now, Art and Ellie can give Roger $20,000 each year tax free. Your lightning mathematical sense no doubt tells you the Dodgers can give Roger only 10% of the business in the first year. Your lightning mathematical sense is wrong.

MINORITY DISCOUNT

Remarkably, Uncle Sam allows the value of a minority interest to be discounted. The theory is that the minority interest is worth less because it is subject to the control of the majority owners. This is true even if the majority owners, to wit: Art and Ellie, happen to be the parents of the minority owner, to wit: Roger.

How much less? That is for an appraiser to determine. A 20% discount for a minority interest is not unusual. In that case, the Dodgers could give more than 10% of the business to Roger the first year and still be within their $20,000 annual exclusion. And that's not all.

MARKETABILITY DISCOUNT

As in many families, there is a certain amount of friction between Ellie and her daughter-in-law (Roger's wife). In fact, Ellie has mentioned with great feeling (not to mention alliteration) that she would "first fry in hell" before letting Roger's wife get her "fat little fingers" into the family business. Therefore, the Dodgers have asked their Clever Attorney to draft an agreement giving them the right to buy back Roger's interest at a set price if he dies before they do. This buy-sell agreement eliminates the risk that Roger's wife will get involved in the business. It also further reduces the value of the gift to Roger, since this restriction makes Roger's interest less marketable. This in turn allows the Dodgers to give to Roger an even greater percentage of the business and still stay within their $20,000 annual exclusion.

THE ENTITY

The form of the Dodgers' business is important. For example, if the business is conducted as a general partnership, the gift to Roger will make him a general partner. As such he will have unlimited personal liability for partnership debts. Roger may be reluctant to accept this risk. Roger will also have a voice in the management of the business. Art may be unwilling to accept this risk.

If the business is a limited partnership, by law Roger can have no management authority. If the business is a corporation, Art can limit Roger's authority by giving him only non-voting stock. In both cases, and in the case of a limited liability company as well, Roger's liability will be limited to the value of his investment.

In the next chapter I'm going to reveal something very personal about Uncle Sam that may shock you. It may also save you taxes.

Gambling
with Uncle Sam

You may find this hard to believe, but Uncle Sam is an incurable gambler. (Remember, you read it here first.) He has joined Gamblers Anonymous and tried numerous expensive cures (all at taxpayer expense), but to no avail. Fortunately, taxpayers can sometimes win bets with Uncle Sam. So if you, too, occasionally like to "play the ponies," pay close attention to what I'm about to tell you.

Several years ago, just when it appeared Uncle Sam had finally kicked the habit, he fell off the wagon with a thud and offered taxpayers a betting proposition that many found irresistible. Of course, the Artful Dodger jumped at the chance to win a nickel off Uncle Sam. Here's how.

THE PROPOSITION

Art's residence, Chez Dodger, is worth $500,000. If Art leaves the residence to his son, Roger, it will be taxed in Art's estate when he dies. Instead of leaving the residence to Roger, Uncle Sam allows Art to transfer the residence into a qualified personal residence trust (known by tax experts and in gambling circles as a QPRT). Art gets to live in the residence for as many years as he chooses. Let's say Art chooses eight years. After eight years, ownership of the residence must pass to Roger.

Here's the gamble: Assuming Art is age 60, if he lives eight years or more he wins. Art has made a gift to Roger of the residence, but the value of the gift is discounted to about $260,000 to take into account the eight years Art can continue to live there. (This value will vary depending on the interest rate used by Uncle Sam, which changes monthly.) Sure, Art has used up $260,000 of his $650,000 exemption. But in return he has removed a $500,000 residence, plus any appreciation occurring after the gift, from his taxable estate.

If Art doesn't survive the eight years, Uncle Sam wins. The residence falls back into Art's estate where it is taxed at 100% of its value on the date of Art's death. It's as if the qualified personal residence trust had never existed.

The trick, obviously, is for Art to guess right in choosing the number of years he can live in the residence. The more years he chooses, the greater the discount. For example, if Art had chosen ten years, the gift would have been valued at about $220,000. If Art gets too piggy, however, and picks 15 years, he may not survive that long, and he will lose his bet with Uncle Sam.

SOME DETAILS

Art, always the skeptic, has a number of questions:

"What if I survive the eight years but don't want to leave my residence?"

In that case, Art can continue to live in the residence as long as he is willing to pay Roger a fair rent. Paying rent will further reduce Art's taxable estate. And Roger, under the implicit threat of disinheritance, will not be inclined to serve Art with a notice terminating his tenancy.

"Will this plan work with any other assets?"

Yes, Art can also put one other residence, such as his mountain cabin, into a separate qualified personal residence trust. But that's it; only two per customer.

"What if I later decide to sell my residence?"

The trust can sell Art's residence and reinvest the proceeds in a replacement residence. The trustee has two years, at most, however, to buy a replacement residence.

Watch out! As this book goes to print Uncle Sam is threatening to do away with qualified personal residence trusts, so they just might go the way of the Dodo.

Next, let's see if we can apply the same concept to gifts of income-producing property.

Halfway House for Big Givers

Once every few months the Artful Dodger locks the door to his study, unlocks the lower left-hand desk drawer, and removes a wad of corporate bonds. Art loves these corporate bonds. He loves the heft of the scissors as they cut out the tiny coupons. He loves the engraved pictures of men with Herculean physiques holding aloft locomotives belching smoke. And those of naked goddesses (20 pounds overweight by today's standards—just right by Art's) looking imperious as lightning bolts stream from their fingertips.

What Art does not love, however, is the thought that these bonds will be taxed in his estate. True, it makes sense to give them to Roger and the little Dickens, er, Dodgers. But Art cannot bear to part with these icons of American enterprise, at least not just now.

How can Art give these bonds to his family members yet still keep them? (No, this is not one of those riddles the Elizabethans were simply wild about. There really is a way.)

THE GIFT WITH STRINGS

Art can give the bonds away but retain the right to receive the income from the bonds for a period of years he can choose. For example, if Art has $100,000 of Black, Inc. bonds paying 10%, he can choose to receive the stream of income from these bonds for ten years. After that, the bonds must pass, income and all, to Roger and the little Dodgers.

Actually, what Art must do is transfer his bonds into a grantor retained annuity trust (GRAT) or a grantor retained unitrust (GRUT). GRATs and GRUTs (in addition to being the most revolting acronyms you will find in this book) are sort of halfway houses for people who, like Art, are not quite ready to make an immediate gift.

A GRAT will pay Art 10% of the original value of the bonds each year for 10 years. The annual payment will always be the same.

A GRUT will pay Art 10% of the value of the bonds determined each year. Therefore, the annual payment will vary depending on the fluctuations of the bond market.

With some limitations, Art can choose the percentage he wishes to withdraw as long as it is at least 5% per year.

THE DISCOUNT

But what is the point of all this? The point is that Uncle Sam reduces the amount of the gift by the value of the income interest Art retains. Therefore, by transferring the bonds into a GRAT or a GRUT, Art uses up less of his lifetime exemption than had he made a gift of the bonds outright or died with the bonds in his estate.

For example, Uncle Sam will value $100,000 of bonds transferred to a ten-year GRAT at only $28,000 after deducting for Art's income interest. If Art had chosen a term of 20 years, the gift would be valued at $7,500; if he had chosen 25 years, the gift would have no value and Art would have transferred $100,000 out of his estate without using up one dime of his exemption! (The exact value of the gift depends on an interest rate established by Uncle Sam, which changes monthly.)

A BIGGER DISCOUNT

Even more exciting to Art is the prospect of transferring his bed-and-breakfast, Dodger Lodge, to a GRAT or a GRUT, because the lodge produces greater cash flow than does a bond and, unlike a bond, can be expected to appreciate. The discount is bigger because the cash flow allows Art to pay himself a higher percentage each year. And any appreciation after the date of the transfer escapes tax in Art's estate.

One problem with GRATs and GRUTs is that if Art does not survive the ten years (or his chosen term), most if not all of the value of the asset will be included in his estate.

This bit of tax exotica may not be for most folks, but for those of you who just can't let go, it could be just the thing.

Are you charitably disposed? In tax planning, though good deeds are their own reward, Uncle Sam sweetens the pot.

Doing Well
by Doing Good

Look around you. The opportunities for charitable giving are everywhere. Children are going hungry, libraries are closed on weekends, high schools are without orchestras or computer labs. Not that any of this does much to soften the obdurate heart of the Artful Dodger. But when Art considers the tax savings that can result from charitable gifts, that same heart softens ever so slightly.

Whether you are truly motivated by a desire to make this world a better place or, like Art, interested mostly in saving taxes, you should know the basics of charitable giving.

LIFETIME GIFTS

As you all know, charitable gifts of cash are fully deductible. The fair market value of noncash gifts is also deductible. (Certain limitations apply to so few of us that I am not going to bore you with these details.) This gives rise to opportunities in the case of appreciated assets. Take Art, for example.

Years ago Art made a killing in the stock market. In just a few years, the value of his 100 shares of Black, Inc. went from $100 to $10,000. Art has heard a rumor that Black, Inc. may soon be showing some red ink and he wants to bail out.

To buy peace at home, he also feels compelled to make a charitable gift to Ellie's favorite charity. If he sells the stock, he will pay income tax on the gain of $9,900 (the difference between his cost and the sales price), which at Art's tax bracket of 39% (state and federal) will leave him $7,228. If he then donates this sum to charity, the tax saving on this gift will amount to only $2,819.

If, on the other hand, Art simply gives the Black, Inc. stock to Ellie's favorite charity, he will avoid paying any income tax on the gain and can deduct the entire $10,000. Art's tax saving now will be $3,900. The point is simple: If you have invested wisely (or luckily), give the asset, not the proceeds.

GIFTS OF TANGIBLE PERSONAL PROPERTY

Borne aloft on a wave of munificence (or greed, if you prefer), Art rushes to his garage and surfaces with the brass spittoon he bought at auction 20 years ago for ten bucks. It is now worth $500. How many of you think he can donate it to charity and claim a $500 deduction on his tax return? How many of you think he can't? How many of you just don't give a damn?

The answer, for those of you who do care, is maybe he can and maybe he can't. If he gives the spittoon to the local SPCA, which turns around, sells it, and spends the $500 on dog biscuits, Art can deduct only the ten bucks he originally paid. If, however, he gives it to the local history society, which displays the spittoon as part of its collection of really repulsive 19th century artifacts, Art can deduct $500. Why? Because he can deduct the value (rather than the cost) of a gift of tangible personal property *only* if the charity can be expected to use the item in a manner related to its function. It is tax distinctions like this that cause one to wonder if Uncle Sam isn't a roaring loony.

GIFTS OF LIFE INSURANCE

Art has an old $25,000 life insurance policy naming Ellie as the beneficiary. Ellie doesn't really need insurance protection any more. If Art gives the policy to charity, he can deduct the value of the policy on his income tax return and the charity will get the proceeds at Art's death.

Ellie thinks this is a great idea since her favorite charity will eventually end up with $25,000. Art thinks it's a great idea too, because of the tax deduction and because, frankly, the insurance on his life wasn't doing him much good anyway.

And there's one more advantage. A gift of life insurance to charity increases the likelihood that, at your death, your survivors will be truly grief stricken.

GIFTS AT DEATH

The value of a bequest to charity is deductible for estate tax purposes. When Ellie and Art are both gone, Ellie wants to leave $100,000 to charity. If she is in a 50% estate tax bracket, Uncle Sam will, in effect, contribute half the gift.

Having whetted their appetites, it is now time for the Clever Attorney to introduce the Dodgers to the sine qua non of charitable opportunities.

Doing Still Better

The other day the Artful Dodger had quite a shock. His Clever Attorney suggested the possibility of Art's making a substantial gift to charity. Since Art's prior charitable generosity has been limited to buying single boxes of Girl Scout cookies, Art wondered if the suggestion might be the result of a two-martini lunch. But by the time Art's Clever Attorney had finished explaining the tax advantages of this type of charitable giving, Art's cold heart had turned downright eleemosynary.

THE PROBLEM

Art owns a rental unit worth $500,000 that he purchased for peanuts many years ago. Unfortunately, it brings in only $1,250 in monthly rent. Art wants to sell the property and invest the proceeds in investments producing a higher rate of return. After paying capital gains tax on the sale, however, Art will have only $355,000 left to invest. To add insult to injury, at Art's death the $355,000 will be taxed in Art's estate. Art's son, Roger, will end up receiving a measly $177,500.

THE CHARITABLE SOLUTION

There is an alternative to this depressing scenario, especially if Art would prefer to see tax dollars flow to charity instead of into Uncle Sam's pocket. For Uncle Sam is uncharacteristically charitable to the taxpayer who is charitable.

Instead of selling his rental, Art can set up a charitable remainder trust. Art then transfers the rental property into the trust. When the trust sells the property, it pays no capital gains tax and the entire $500,000 can be invested in more productive assets. Art can direct that the trustee pay him a stated amount from the trust (minimum 5%) annually. He also can direct, at his death, that the trustee continue to pay this amount to his wife, Ellie, for her life. But on Ellie's death, what's left in the trust must pass to the charity of Art's choice.

Art can choose to have the trust pay him each year 5%, for example, of the original value of the trust. This is called a charitable remainder annuity trust. Or he can choose to have the trust pay him each year 5% of the value of the trust computed annually. This is called a charitable remainder unitrust.

Until recently, Art could have extended the payout over Roger's life. But Uncle Sam has tightened the screws on charitable trusts such that now it is usually not possible to include children.

ADVANTAGES

The primary advantage of a charitable remainder trust is that Art can invest the entire sales proceeds from his rental unit for the benefit of his family without any attrition due to capital gains tax.

There are other benefits as well. Art can take a charitable deduction on his income tax return, which will shelter some of the money the trust pays him each year. The amount of the deduction depends on the value of the eventual gift to charity as computed by Uncle Sam. For example, if the trust terminates on Art's death, the deduction is bigger than if the trust continues on for Ellie's life. Likewise, the smaller the percentage payout Art chooses, the bigger the deduction. And if Art can't use up all the deduction in one year, he can carry it forward up to five years.

Also, the trust will pay no capital gains tax on the sale of the assets in which it has invested. Thus, if the trust sells Intermittent Gas and Electricity, Inc. at a gain, the entire proceeds can be reinvested.

Art is still concerned that Roger will lose some of his inheritance. No problem. Art can use some of the money he receives from the trust to buy a life insurance policy on Art's life, naming Roger as the beneficiary. In fact, Art can transfer ownership of the policy to Roger. That way, at Art's death the proceeds will not be taxable in Art's estate.

One other advantage pleases Art, although he won't admit it. He and Ellie most likely will receive immediate public recognition for their generosity. All of which is better than a few stale Girl Scout cookies.

In the next chapter, I will answer the question, "Do you need a will?" (Hint: When an attorney asks this question, you can bet the farm it's purely rhetorical.)

CHAPTER 16

To Will or Not to Will

So far we have discussed some pretty exotic tax-planning techniques. In this chapter, we're going back to basics. Not everybody has an estate large enough to require tax planning. (Nor does everyone, like the Artful Dodger, have a borderline personality when it comes to trying to avoid taxes.)

Let's start with the most fundamental question of all.

DO YOU NEED A WILL?

If you die without a will, you die intestate. No, this doesn't mean all your earthly booty is forfcited to the state. It does mean your property passes by intestate succession. This is the law that, in effect, writes your will for you if you don't have one. It provides for the distribution of your estate to the people whom the state assumes you would have chosen. Different states have different intestacy laws.

For example, if you are married and die in a community property state, chances are your half of the community property passes to your surviving spouse and your separate property passes to both your surviving spouse and your children. If you are single, without children, your property probably passes to your parents equally.

This may not be so bad. But it also may not be what you want. Your will (or your living trust) ensures your property passes to the people you choose.

WHO'S IN CHARGE?

In your will you can name your personal representative. This is the person who will have the responsibility of administering your estate. And you can waive the requirement for a bond. (A bond is like an insurance policy that protects your estate if the representative disappears in your Ferrari Testarossa.)

You should waive bond if you have complete trust in your chosen representative. This is important since bonds are expensive. (Today, a bond on a $750,000 estate costs about $950 per year.)

If you die intestate, your representative will be appointed by the court, and bond may be required even if your representative is a family member.

The choice of your representative can be important. Normally it will be a family member. However, if Thanksgiving Day in your family has come to be known as the "annual brawl," you should consider someone outside the family or even a professional representative such as a bank trust department.

ALTERNATIVES TO A WILL

Not all property passes by your will. For example, property held in joint tenancy passes to the surviving joint tenant outside your will. Therefore, if you hold title to Bleakacre in joint tenancy with your girlfriend, Marilyn, at your death it will pass automatically to her. (If you also have left Bleakacre in your will to your other girlfriend, Carolyn, you have set the stage for the type of nasty lawsuit that allows attorneys to send their kids to private schools.)

Retirement benefits, life insurance, and some investments (like government bonds) that are payable at your death to a person you have designated will not pass by your will. Nor will bank accounts held in trust for another or, of course, assets held in a living trust.

So it is possible for you to direct where your property will go without having a will. This is risky, however. For if the other joint tenant of Bleakacre or the beneficiary of your life insurance dies before you (or in a common disaster with you), this property will pass by intestate succession at your death.

I don't mean to scare you, but in the next chapter there will be a test of your probate I.Q.

Test Your Probate I.Q.

In a recent survey, average Americans were given the following multiple-choice test:

"Probate is:
a. A really nasty toxin.
b. A sexually transmitted disease.
c. The judicial process for the orderly distribution of an estate."

A majority of respondents guessed wrong and no wonder. You no doubt have heard probate talked about as if it were the fifth horseman of the apocalypse. Yet, if you're like most people, you probably don't have much of an idea just what probate is.

NONPROBATE PROPERTY

For starters, the following property does not have to be probated:

(a) Property held in joint tenancy;
(b) Life insurance proceeds (unless you named your probate estate as the beneficiary);
(c) Assets, such as retirement accounts (like IRAs) and government bonds, that are payable on death to a person you name;
(d) All assets passing outright from one spouse to another; and
(e) Assets held in a living trust.

THE WAY IT WORKS

The rest of your property is subject to probate. Let's take a short stroll through probate to see what it's really all about. Probate procedures differ from state to state. Generically most probates are something like this:

A probate proceeding is started by the person you named in your will as your personal representative. If you didn't get around to making a will, just about anybody can start the proceeding (even one of your creditors) but preference is given to your spouse and your relatives.

The person seeking to be your representative files a petition for probate in the Superior Court. He or she then publishes a notice in a local newspaper, which informs your creditors that they must file their claims and informs the public of the date of the first hearing. This notice must also be sent to all the beneficiaries named in your will, as well as to your next of kin.

At the first hearing, the judge appoints the person who will have the responsibility of managing your estate. This person is called an executor if he was named in your will, or an administrator if you died without a will. (If the person is a she and you are either a Latin scholar or a snob, she is called an executrix or an administratrix.) The term "personal representative" covers both.

Unless it is challenged, the judge will admit your will to probate and order letters of administration issued to your personal representative. These letters are your representative's written authority to act for the estate. Your creditors have a limited time (often four months) from the date these letters are issued to file a claim against your estate for money due, or they will be out of luck.

This cutoff of creditors' claims is an important benefit of probate. For example, if you are a doctor, a lawyer, or other professional, malpractice claims that are not filed on time are forever barred. Moreover, your representative can choose to probate both halves of the community property, thus protecting all community property, such as the family residence, from future claims.

Just what exactly does your representative do to probate your estate? Read on, MacDuff.

More about Probate

I know a lot of you readers, in a state of nail-biting anxiety, have rushed ahead to learn more about the probate process. Here, then, is the second installment.

THE INVENTORY AND APPRAISAL

Your personal representative's first task is to inventory the property of the estate and have it appraised, usually by the probate referee. These values are used on your estate tax return if one is required.

These values also establish the new tax basis of all estate assets. For example, the vacation cottage you purchased for $50,000 (your original tax basis) will get a new basis of $500,000, the value at the date of your death. Your beneficiaries will pay capital gains tax on only those sales proceeds over $500,000.

SIMPLIFIED PROCEDURE

It used to be that every time your representative wanted to do anything important, he or she had to go to court for authority. Now, in many states your representative takes most actions such as selling property, investing estate assets, entering into contracts, and the like without going to court. Instead, he or she needs only to notify your beneficiaries in advance of any such action. If none objects, he or she can go ahead.

HELP FROM THE JUDGE

Occasionally your representative may run into a problem that requires court assistance. For example, let's say your will provides, "To my good friend, Art Dodger, I leave $10,000 so he can take good care of my pit bull, Vise Grips." Unfortunately, "Visey" trotted off to his reward years ago. Art claims he should get the money, anyway. Your children, who get the rest of your estate, are adamant: "No Visey, no $10,000."

Your representative can request the court to instruct him or her just what to do. Probate judges, who handle scores of probate cases each week, are adept at solving problems such as this. And your representative, in following the judge's instruction, is protected from personal liability.

FINANCIAL STUFF

During probate your representative receives all income, pays all expenses, invests surplus cash, and generally manages your estate. He or she also files your last personal income tax returns along with your estate's income tax returns, known as fiduciary returns.

If your gross estate exceeds the amount of your personal exemption ($650,000 in 1999, increasing to $1,000,000 by 2006), your representative must also file an estate tax return within nine months of your death. After the time for filing creditors' claims has expired and after your estate tax return has been filed, your estate can be closed.

WINDING THINGS UP

To wind things up, your representative files a petition for distribution in the probate court. Unless waived by the beneficiaries, your representative must attach an itemized accounting showing all assets at the beginning of the probate and at its end, all income and expenses, and all gains and losses on sales. The tricky part, of course, is that the accounting must balance.

The representative also requests approval of his or her fees and the probate attorney's fees. Your representative and the probate attorney are each entitled to a probate fee the amount of which varies from state to state. In California, for example, the fee for estates under $1,000,000 is equal to 2% of the gross value of the estate plus $1,150. The probate fee is 1% on anything over $1,000,000 and (I realize this is getting somewhat academic) 1/2% on anything over $10,000,000.

Your representative, especially if a family member, will probably waive this fee. Attorney's fees also may be less than the probate fee if negotiated at the beginning of the probate proceeding.

Finally, your representative sets out how the estate will be distributed. Once this petition is approved, your representative will distribute your estate and be discharged.

In the next chapter, I will tell you something that just may help you win your next bar bet.

The Living Trust:
Fact and Fiction

Perhaps you've seen ads similar to the one that has appeared in many newspapers, in which a self-styled "money expert" invites you to attend his "Money Power Workshop." Here he promises to show you how living trusts can "reduce or eliminate estate taxes." This is pure eyewash.

THE FICTION

Living trusts save estate taxes. Not so! No living trust has ever saved a penny of estate taxes. These money experts, along with others who make their living selling living trusts like washing detergent, often confuse the public by making this claim.

The truth is, a living trust is a valuable estate planning tool you should consider. But not for the wrong reasons.

THE FACT

A living trust is a will substitute. In the typical living trust, an individual transfers all of his or her property to himself or herself as trustee of a living trust. Although a living trust doesn't save taxes, it does avoid probate.

PROBATE FEES

As you know, probate is the judicial process for the orderly distribution of an estate. The problem with probate is probate fees.

Your attorney and your personal representative are each entitled to a probate fee, which is usually set by statute in each state. The fee is often the same for each. Your personal representative, if a member of your family, will probably waive the fee. Therefore, in most cases only the attorney's fee should concern you. For example, in a $500,000 estate the attorney's fee, depending on where you live (or, actually, where you die) might range from $10,000 to $15,000. (As we will see in a few paragraphs, however, this fee is not carved in marble.)

Attorneys may also charge extraordinary fees for services that go beyond the normal probate duties. Most judges, however, are loathe to allow extraordinary fees unless the attorney can make a compelling case that they are justified.

If you have a living trust, there will be no probate and, ergo, no probate fee at your death. To say a living trust avoids attorney's fees is probably an overstatement. For at your death the successor trustee you name will probably hire an attorney to assist in the administration of your trust. These fees should be significantly less, however, than in the case of a probate.

OTHER ADVANTAGES

In addition to probate avoidance, a living trust offers other advantages. It affords an economical alternative to a conservatorship. In the event of your future incapacity, your successor trustee, rather than a court-appointed conservator, will take over handling your affairs.

If you own real property in another state, a living trust offers a simple method of transferring the property at your death without the need of setting up a probate in a foreign state.

However, a living trust costs more than a will because it is a more complicated document and because, after executing the trust, you must transfer your assets into it.

Believe it or not, probate actually has some advantages. For example, in some cases probate affords a simpler way to transfer assets to your beneficiaries. And in some community property states your representative can protect *both* halves of the community property from creditors' claims that are not filed on time.

A MODEST PROPOSAL

For those who are not sure they want a living trust, there is a middle ground. In your will you can advise your personal representative that probate fees, though set by statute, are negotiable. You can instruct your personal representative to negotiate probate fees before hiring a probate attorney. You can even point out that your personal representative need not hire the attorney who drafted your will to probate your estate. In the case of a well-organized estate, your personal representative should be able to negotiate a substantial reduction of the normal probate fee.

For those inclined towards a living trust, you have some work to do. Stay tuned.

Implementing
Your Living Trust

If Art and Ellie decide a living trust is just the thing for them, there are some steps they should take to make sure the thing actually works.

TRANSFERRING ASSETS
INTO THE TRUST

Signing a living trust is only half the job. To avoid probate, the Dodgers must also transfer their assets into the trust. From now on the Dodgers will own their assets not as Art and Ellie Dodger, just plain folks, but as Art and Ellie Dodger, co-trustees of the Dodger living trust. (This is O.K. as far as it goes, but will probably not get them a better table at the local French restaurant.) Some assets are a little more difficult to transfer than others.

CHEZ DODGER

The Dodgers must sign a deed transferring their home, Chez Dodger, and any other real estate to the trust. In those states that exempt a transfer to a living trust from property tax re-assessment, a form should be filed with the tax assessor claiming this exemption. Also, if Chez Dodger has a mortgage, out of an abundance of caution Art may want to check with the lender, to make sure the transfer won't trigger a payoff demand. (Though a theoretical possibility, it is a rare lender that would be so dastardly as to do this.)

CLOSELY HELD BUSINESSES

If Art holds an interest in a partnership or a closely held corporation that has not yet gone bankrupt, he should make sure there are no transfer restrictions. If there are, the other partners or shareholders (who may be contemplating a living trust for themselves) will probably waive the restrictions and permit the transfer.

STOCKS AND BONDS

This tip alone is worth the cost of this book. There are two ways to transfer securities into a living trust, the hard way and the easy way. The hard way is to write to the transfer agent of each stock or bond requesting forms necessary to put the security into your trust. In the fullness of time, after many letters back and forth, you will eventually accomplish your goal. The easy way is to put the securities into a brokerage account, then simply change the name of the account to the trust. This takes approximately five minutes.

HEIRLOOMS

Family heirlooms, furniture, jewelry, antiques, artwork, and the like can be transferred into your trust by a simple assignment like the one in Appendix D. Be sure the assignment includes property you own now *and* property you may acquire in the future.

EXCEPTIONS

Not all assets must be transferred into the living trust. For example, your retirement accounts and IRAs cannot be held by a trust. But don't worry. Since these accounts pass to your designated beneficiary, they will escape probate. Likewise, life insurance (which names a beneficiary other than your estate), joint tenancy accounts, and certain other assets that are payable on your death to a named beneficiary need not be transferred into your trust since they will avoid probate anyway.

TAX CONSIDERATIONS

If you were to tell Uncle Sam you had a living trust, he would probably say "Huh?" because, as you now know, living trusts have nothing to do with taxes and consequently are of no interest to Uncle Sam. This is good news in a way. Art and Ellie do not have to file a separate tax return for the trust (as long as both are alive), and they can continue to use their own social security numbers on bank and securities accounts even after they have transferred them into the trust.

COMMUNITY VERSUS SEPARATE PROPERTY

In community property states, most living trusts provide that transferring property into the trust will not change its character. In other words, community property will remain community property and separate property will remain separate property. Art and Ellie should identify and segregate separate and community property in the trust. This will ensure favorable tax treatment of all community property (see chapter 24). And Art and Ellie will each continue to own and control his or her separate property.

THE POUR-OVER WILL

Just because the Dodgers execute a living trust doesn't mean they don't need a will. Art and Ellie also should execute simple wills bequeathing their estates to their living trust. This type of will is referred to as a pour-over will because it pours over into the living trust any assets inadvertently left out. It may take a probate proceeding to accomplish this, however, so the pour-over will should be regarded as a safety net rather than an alternative to physically transferring the assets into the living trust.

The fruits of the Dodgers' labors unfortunately will only be harvested upon the death of one of them, which, by general acclamation, will be Art.

CHAPTER 21

Morte d'Arthur

We will now go back, as they say, to the future—to a time 20 years from now. Art has passed on. Ellie must now undertake the administration of the living trust. If all the Dodgers' assets have been transferred into the living trust, Ellie will never see the inside of a probate court, because no probate proceeding is necessary. If not . . .

WHOOPS!

What if Ellie discovers that Art never got around to transferring his stock in Black, Inc. into the trust? She has several options:

- If Black, Inc. is listed in the trust as an asset, in some states it is possible to file a simple petition with the court requesting an order transferring the stock into the trust.
- Or if the value of Black, Inc. is less than a certain amount (for example, $100,000 in California), most states provide a simple procedure for Ellie to transfer the stock into the trust without a probate.
- If none of these procedures is available, Ellie must go through an entire probate proceeding for this one asset. This is why it is so important to be sure your trust is fully funded.

Now that Ellie has taken steps to make sure Art's trust is fully funded, there are other important matters she must attend to.

CREDITORS' CLAIMS

In probate, a creditor must file its claim within a specified time. If it doesn't, its claim is cut off. It used to be there was no similar protection afforded living trusts. Now in many states Ellie has the right to publish a notice to Art's creditors in the newspaper. And just like in probate, Art's creditors (and we certainly hope the Clever Attorney is not one of them) must file claims with Ellie, as the trustee, within the time stated in the notice or the claim is barred. Even if Ellie doesn't think Art has any creditors, she should take advantage of this simple procedure. For if 2020 is as sue-happy an age as this one, no one, not even Art, is immune.

NOTIFICATION

In some states Ellie has a duty to notify Art's heirs and the beneficiaries of his trust of his death and provide them with a copy of the trust upon request. This is true even though Ellie is the only one who has the right to receive distributions from the living trust.

FILING ESTATE TAX
RETURN

If the Dodgers have done their tax planning carefully, there will be no estate tax payable on Art's death. However, if the value of Art's property exceeds his lifetime exemption (assuming there is such a thing in the year 2020), Ellie must file an estate tax return within nine months of Art's death. Art's property must be appraised for estate tax purposes. This appraised value will also establish Ellie's new tax basis. Remember: Even though Art owned only one-half of any community property, both halves of the community will get a new tax basis. If these assets have increased in value, Ellie will pay less capital gains taxes when she sells these assets later.

FILING INCOME TAX
RETURNS

Ellie must now start reporting income generated by Art's assets on separate income tax returns. Ellie may be able to save income taxes by electing to file Art's returns on a fiscal rather than a calendar year. She should be sure to discuss this option with her accountant.

FUNDING THE QTIP
AND BYPASS TRUSTS

Finally, Ellie must divide Art's property between the QTIP and the bypass trusts. Subtrust funding is technical, can be complicated, and, fortunately for you, is way beyond the purview of this little book. Suffice it to say, Ellie must get professional help from her Clever Attorney or Clever Accountant. Once Ellie has determined which of Art's assets go into each trust, she must transfer Art's assets from the living trust to the QTIP and the bypass trusts. This procedure is similar to the one she and Art went through 20 years ago when they originally transferred their assets into their living trust. From now on Ellie is trustee of not one but three trusts, Art's QTIP and bypass trusts and her trust (containing Ellie's assets that remain in the original living trust). She must account for these trusts separately and she must never, never mix the assets of one with another.

Next let's look inside an estate planner's toolbox where we'll find some handy little tools that will fix future problems.

Your Estate Planning Toolbox

In this chapter we're going to take a break from taxes. (Buck up! We'll return to them soon enough.) Instead, I'm going to tell you about documents you may want to include in your estate plan. Think of these documents as tools in your estate planning toolbox. At least one of these tools may be just the right thing to fix a future problem.

Warning! These forms are presented by way of example only. Do not use them without the advice of your own Clever Attorney.

DURABLE POWER OF ATTORNEY
FOR HEALTH CARE

This document (Appendix E) allows you to appoint the person of your choice to make health care decisions for you if you are unable to do so. At the same time, you can designate that your life not be artificially prolonged if your condition is irreversible, or alternatively that every measure be undertaken to keep you alive. If you want to specify your desires regarding specific life-sustaining procedures, you can attach a Statement of Desires (Appendix F) to your durable power. You may also consent to the donation of your body parts for medical or scientific purposes.

The advantage of this document is that it invests the person of your choice with the power to monitor and control the course of your medical treatment when you can't. If there is someone to whom you are willing to delegate this authority, do it!

DIRECTIVE TO PHYSICIANS

This document, sometimes referred to as a living will (Appendix G), is useful if there is nobody to whom you want to delegate your health care decisions. It directs your physician to withhold life-sustaining treatment if you are in an irreversible coma.

DURABLE GENERAL
POWER OF ATTORNEY

This document appoints another person to conduct your affairs for you. You can choose to have it take effect immediately (Appendix H-1) or only in the event of your future incompetency (Appendix H-2). In cases of temporary disability, it is an economical alternative to a conservatorship.

If you have a living trust, it is important that you also execute a power of attorney. It can be used to transfer assets you might have overlooked into the trust if you become unable to do so. And if your trust allows, it can be used to amend your trust after your incompetency if necessary, for example, to take advantage of the latest tax reform act.

You can even give your spouse the right to make annual exclusion gifts on your behalf to your children and grandchildren long after you no longer have legal capacity to do so yourself.

COMMUNITY PROPERTY AFFIDAVIT

If you live in a community property state, this simple document (Appendix I) can pay huge dividends. It converts assets held in joint tenancy to community property. In chapter 24 we will discuss the advantages of holding property that has gone up in value as community property. For you westerners, this is one of the most important things you will learn in this book!

NOMINATION OF CONSERVATOR

As we will see in chapter 32, a conservatorship is a judicial proceeding in which the court appoints an individual or an institution to handle your affairs if you are unable to do so yourself. Did you know you can nominate your own conservator even if you may never need a conservatorship? You can nominate a conservator in your Durable Power of Attorney for Health Care or in a separate Nomination of Conservator (Appendix J).

In most conservatorships the conservator must post a bond. The bond protects the conservatorship from loss if the conservator takes a powder to Mexico with the conservatorship assets. Bonds can be expensive. Therefore, when your nominee is a trusted relative or a close family friend, you may wish to waive the bond requirement in your nomination.

In the next chapter we will treat with a subject that most of us would just as soon avoid—planning for our untimely death.

CHAPTER

Providing for Your Orphans

Small wonder we procrastinate when it comes to planning our estates. To plan an estate is to concede to our mortality; it is to hear at our back "time's winged chariot hurrying near."

Worse yet, to plan well we must advert to unpleasant eventualities, such as an untimely death, that may leave young children orphaned. Plan we must, however, for the consequences of not doing so can be unfortunate.

GUARDIANSHIP OF THE PERSON

As long as either you or your spouse is living, the surviving spouse will most likely provide for the needs of any minor children. On the death of the surviving spouse, however, or if both you and your spouse die in a common disaster, the court will appoint a guardian of the person of your minor children. This guardian will have the responsibility of raising your children. In your will you should designate the person or persons you want to assume this task. Remember, if you appoint a married couple as guardians, you should state what is to happen if the couple separates. And you should discuss the guardianship with the persons you name to make sure they are willing to accept the responsibility.

GUARDIANSHIP OF THE ESTATE

If you leave property outright to minor children either by will (or living trust), joint tenancy, or life insurance, the court will appoint a guardian of your children's estate who will have the responsibility of managing your children's property until they reach the age of majority.

You can designate this person in your will. Estate guardianships, however, have disadvantages. For example, a guardianship bond will be required, which can be expensive. Also, the guardian must file periodic accountings and obtain court approval before making certain sales, investments, or distributions, which can add to the cost.

Most importantly, the estate must be distributed to your child at his or her majority. And if your child dies before reaching majority, the estate will be distributed to the child's heirs. This may not be what you want.

GIFTS IN TRUST

Is there an alternative to a guardianship of the estate? Yes. In your will or your living trust, you can set up a trust for your children. A trust has two major advantages.

First, you have great flexibility in just how you want the trust administered and distributed. For example, you can establish a separate trust for each child that distributes one-half of the property to your child when he or she reaches 25 and the balance at age 30. Or you can provide for a single trust (known as a family pot trust) to be held for the benefit of all your children until the youngest child reaches 21 or whichever age you designate.

Second, if a child dies before the trust terminates, you can direct to whom distribution of the child's share should be made—to the child's spouse, for example, or the child's children, or your other children.

GIFT TO CUSTODIAN

This simple alternative to a trust can also avoid the necessity of a guardianship. You can make a gift in your will to a custodian for your child under the Uniform Transfers to Minors Act. The custodian you appoint can manage your child's estate without any court supervision. This means no bonds, no accountings, and probably no attorneys' fees. And you can delay payment to your child until age 25.

SPECIAL NEEDS TRUST

If you have a disabled child who is receiving or likely to receive public benefit assistance, there is an added concern. A bequest to the child may disqualify the child from receiving that assistance. If allowable in your state, consider leaving the child's bequest to a special needs trust. In this trust, the trustee's authority is limited to providing your child with only those benefits not paid for by public assistance.

The result is that Medicaid, for example, cannot consider the assets of the trust in determining your child's eligibility. And the trustee can provide your child with important assistance not covered by Medicaid, such as a specially equipped vehicle, dental care, rehabilitation, or even a vacation.

In the next chapter you will learn how one simple, inexpensive affidavit can save you lots of income tax.

One More Reason
to Head Out West

If you live in a community property state (namely, Arizona, California, Idaho, Louisiana, Nevada, New Mexico, Texas, Washington, or Wisconsin), the way in which you and your spouse hold title to property has significant income tax consequences. In fact, Uncle Sam, in a rare outburst of generosity, has made tax savings available in community property states that are not available elsewhere. To illustrate how this beneficence can save you taxes, we will turn again to the Artful Dodger, who, as we know, has raised tax avoidance to an art form.

CAPITAL GAINS TAX

You will recall that years ago Art had the foresight to buy 100 shares of Black, Inc. for $100, which has soared in value to $10,000. (If you don't, I'm sure Art will be happy to regale you with the details.) If Art sells the stock, he will pay income tax on the difference between the original cost of $100 (known as his tax basis) and the sales price of $10,000.

If Art dies owning these shares of Black, Inc., however, his original tax basis is "stepped up" to the stock's value (say $10,000) at his death. If Ellie sells Black, Inc. for $10,000 after Art's death, no income tax is payable.

If, instead, Art and Ellie own Black, Inc. as joint tenants, upon either's death, the basis will be stepped up but only as to one-half the difference between the cost basis of $100 and the value at death of $10,000. The new basis will be $5,050 ($100 plus $4,950). If the surviving spouse sells the stock for $10,000, the remaining $4,850 is taxed.

When Art and Ellie told their Clever Attorney they owned Black, Inc. (along with their residence and other appreciated assets) in joint tenancy, the Clever Attorney wouldn't let them out the door until they had signed a Community Property Affidavit (Appendix I) stating that all these joint tenancy assets were really community property. As a result, the situation will be dramatically different on the death of the first spouse. The basis of the stock, as if it had been sprinkled with pixie dust, will be stepped up to $10,000 regardless of whether Art or Ellie is the first to die. If the surviving spouse sells the stock for $10,000, no income tax is payable.

Holding title as community property has one other advantage. On Art's death, for example, since community property assets get a stepped-up tax basis, Ellie will not have to go rooting through Art's business records (located in a cardboard box, God knows where) to try to figure out the original cost of each asset.

HOW TO SAVE IT

Here are some ways you can take advantage of these rules and save income taxes.

(1) Do you and your spouse own a residence? If so, pull out the deed to your residence. Chances are you and your spouse hold title as joint tenants. (This is probably because the person at the title company told you to take title this way.) If your residence has gone up in value, convert it to community property along with any other appreciated joint tenancy property. Just like Art and Ellie, you can do this by executing a simple Community Property Affidavit. This way

the surviving spouse will get a full step up in basis on the death of the other spouse. Be careful, however. If you own joint tenancy assets that have gone down in value, you may not want to change them to community property. A joint tenancy asset that has depreciated gives the surviving spouse a bigger income tax loss than in the case of an asset held as community property. In this case, it is better not to execute an all-inclusive Community Property Affidavit but, instead, to transfer to community property only those assets that have appreciated.

(2) Do you and your spouse each own appreciated separate property? If so, each of you should transfer separate property of equal value to community property. Then no matter which of you dies first, the survivor will get a full step up in basis on all the converted property.

(3) What if you own appreciated separate property but your spouse doesn't? Consider transferring it to community property even if your spouse cannot match the transfer with separate property of his or her own. If your spouse dies before you, you will get a step up in the tax basis on the community property that was formerly your separate property.

Obviously, this strategy raises considerations that go beyond tax planning. You will be making a transfer of your separate property to community property that once made is irrevocable. If you and your spouse divorce, you will doubtless come to regard this bit of tax planning as unenlightened.

For those of you wondering whether to squeeze in one last chapter before bedtime, the answer is "don't," because the next chapter and the two following are among the toughest in this book, so much so they send even the Clever Attorney to the medicine cabinet.

IRA Stands for
Impossible to Readily Apprehend

One hot afternoon Carol, the Clever Attorney's secretary, announced, "Art just dropped by to discuss his IRA." "Send him in," the Clever Attorney sighed as his hand involuntarily groped in his lower desk drawer for the ibuprofen. It was not so much that he minded Art's habit of dropping in unannounced, which he did; it was that Uncle Sam had created a set of rules dealing with IRAs so complex they would be the envy of a Byzantine emperor. And explaining them to Art in the Clever Attorney's Swedish sauna of an office would be no fun.

Almost since Art was in knickers, he has made yearly tax-free contributions to his IRA account. Since this money has been compounding tax free, Art has managed to tuck away more than $1,000,000. Art understands Uncle Sam will tax every penny he withdraws from his IRA at ordinary income tax rates. Art wants to know how he can reduce these income taxes.

NOT TOO SOON AND
NOT TOO LATE

Under normal circumstances, Art cannot take money out of his IRA before he is 59-1/2 without incurring a 10% tax in addition to ordinary income taxes on any premature distributions. Art *must* begin taking the money out when he reaches

70-1/2. If he doesn't, Uncle Sam will exact a penalty equal to 50% of the money Art should have taken out but didn't.

NOT TOO MUCH AND
NOT TOO LITTLE

It used to be that if Art took too much out of his IRA, he had to pay a 15% excise tax on the excess distributions. But no more. Now all Art has to worry about is taking too little. For if he takes too little, Uncle Sam will slap him with a 50% excise tax on the money he should have taken out. At retirement Art has a number of options:

- Art can withdraw all his IRA in a lump sum. Problem is, the money he receives is subject to income tax all at once. "Is there any way I can take out less?" asks Art. Yes . . .

- Art can take the money out over his life expectancy. For example, if Art starts making withdrawals at age 70-1/2, Uncle Sam predicts that Art will live another 16 years, to the ripe age of 86. Art can take out 1/16 of the IRA's value in the first year, and 1/15 of the IRA's value in the second year, and so on until the IRA is fully distributed at age 86. But, Art points out, "I will be out of money by age 86. I intend to live to be 100!" In that case . . .

- Uncle Sam gives Art the option of recalculating his life expectancy each year. When Art reaches age 72, Uncle Sam predicts Art will live even longer, to age 87, in fact. (In insurance jargon Art is "chasing his actuarial tail.") By recalculating, Art can spread his IRA withdrawals over his increasingly greater life expectancy so no matter how long he lives, the pot will never run dry. "That's better, but I want to protect Ellie, too," Art says. Then . . .

- Art can name Ellie as a beneficiary along with him. Since Art and Ellie's joint life expectancies will always be greater than Art's alone, Art can take even less out each year. And if Art chooses, either Ellie's life expectancy, Art's life expectancy, or the life expectancy of both can be recalculated each year to further reduce the withdrawals. "What happens on my death if Ellie survives me?" Art wants to know (at which point the Clever Attorney is wondering when the ibuprofen will kick in). Ellie has three choices:

- Ellie can elect to have the balance of the IRA paid out over the remaining life expectancy of her and Art; however, if Art's life expectancy has been recalculated, it becomes zero at his death and Ellie's withdrawals are computed over her life expectancy alone. Or . . .

- Ellie can "roll over" Art's IRA into her IRA and treat it as her own. Ellie gets a fresh start and has the same withdrawal options as Art did. Ellie can choose Roger as a beneficiary along with her. Now the withdrawals will be based on the joint life expectancies of Ellie and Roger. As long as Ellie is living, however, in calculating the joint life expectancy Roger is deemed to be no more than ten years younger than Ellie.

Since this stuff is pretty technical, I'm going to give you a break here. When you feel up to it, we will take off where we left off, in the next chapter.

IRA Stands for Impossible to Readily Apprehend—Continued

When we left off last time, the Clever Attorney had just explained how Ellie could roll Art's IRA over, get a fresh start, and name Roger as a beneficiary along with her. Art, who to the exasperation of the Clever Attorney is showing not the slightest signs of fatigue, now wants to know, "What happens on Ellie's death?"

Roger, unlike Ellie, does *not* have the right to roll the IRA over into his IRA, but he can begin making withdrawals over *his* life expectancy; however, unlike Art and Ellie, he cannot choose annual recalculation. Moreover, Roger's life expectancy is determined as of the date Ellie starts withdrawing from her IRA.

"What if Ellie dies before I do?" Art asks.

Distributions to Art continue over what's left of the Dodgers' joint life expectancy. But if Ellie's life expectancy was being recalculated, it becomes zero at her death, and distributions will be made based on Art's life expectancy alone.

NAMING A TRUST
AS BENEFICIARY

"Can I provide for Ellie in my IRA but also ensure there will be money left over for Roger?" asks Art. By now Art has almost reached the limits of the Clever Attorney's patience (as well as his Right Guard). But the Clever Attorney perseveres.

Yes. Art has set up a QTIP trust (see chapter 3) for the benefit of Ellie during her lifetime. Art can name his QTIP trust as the beneficiary of his IRA. The QTIP trustee must withdraw all the IRA income and distribute it to Ellie annually, and Ellie must have the right to insist that all assets of the IRA generate reasonable income.

If the trust meets certain technical requirements (which for once in the history of tax planning are not that difficult), Art can make withdrawals over his and Ellie's joint lifetimes just as if he had named Ellie the beneficiary. At Art's death, however, Ellie does not have the roll-over option and what is left in the IRA at her death will be distributed to Roger. Roger, however, must make withdrawals over the remaining joint life expectancy of his parents.

Art can also name his bypass trust (see chapter 4) as beneficiary. This is useful if Art doesn't have enough other assets to fully fund the bypass trust up to the amount of his lifetime exemption. As with the QTIP trust, if the bypass trust is properly drafted, Art can use his and Ellie's life expectancies in spreading out the required distributions.

Finally, if Ellie doesn't need to rely on the IRA for support, Art can name his generation-skipping trust (see chapter 7) as beneficiary. During Art's life, distributions are made to Art over the joint life expectancies of Art and Roger (however, for this calculation Uncle Sam presumes Roger to be only ten years younger than Art). At Art's death, payments will be made to the generation-skipping trust over Roger's life expectancy without a ten-year limitation. The trustee of the generation-skipping trust (probably Roger) can pay to Roger the income from the trust and as much of the principal as is necessary for Roger's support. At Roger's death what is left in the generation-skipping trust will pass to the little Dodgers free of tax in Roger's estate. Art must make sure his IRA contains no more the $1,000,000 at his death or Uncle Sam will sock his beneficiary with the confiscatory generation-skipping tax.

ONE DRAWBACK

There is one problem with naming a trust as Art's IRA beneficiary. The trust will pay income taxes on any income not distributed annually. And trusts pay more income taxes than individuals. For example, a trust reaches a 39% tax bracket with income of only $8,000, while Art doesn't reach this bracket until he has earned income of $278,000.

"So what would you do if you were I?" asked Art. The Clever Attorney had finally had enough. "If I were you, I would invite me across the street to Mac's Tea Room to sample some of Mac's Vin Tres Ordinaire," replied the Clever Attorney. And Art did.

The IRA,
Philosophically Speaking

In the cool recesses of Mac's, two glasses of plonk, drained to the lees, gradually restored the Clever Attorney to conviviality, and at Art's urging he began to discuss some broader strategies that apply to Art's retirement planning.

THE NAME OF THE GAME
IS STRETCH OUT

In retirement planning, Art's goal is to stretch out IRA distributions over as many years as possible. (Unless, of course, Art or Ellie needs more of the IRA for their own needs.) This is because IRAs compound tax free, and the longer Art can keep his IRA compounding tax free, the more of it will be available for eventual distribution.

THE DOUBLE WHAMMY

All good things, including tax-free compounding, must someday come to an end. Art's IRA is subject to both income tax and estate tax. The effect of the two taxes can be devastating. For example, let's assume Art names Roger as the beneficiary of his million-dollar IRA, and at Art's death, Roger, who cannot wait to get his hands on the money, withdraws the whole thing. After paying estate and income taxes out of the IRA, Roger could end up with as little as $174,000.

Let's look at some strategies to help Art avoid this unhappy result.

THE SPOUSAL ROLLOVER

Naming Ellie as Art's beneficiary works great if Ellie survives Art. For Ellie can roll over Art's IRA and name a new beneficiary such as Roger or, better yet, the little Dodgers, thus stretching distributions out over several generations. But if Ellie dies first, there is a problem. For Art cannot use the life expectancies of either Roger or the little Dodgers to stretch out distributions. Therefore, if Ellie doesn't need the IRA, Art should consider naming Roger as his beneficiary (or a generation-skipping trust). Or better still, Art can name the little Dodgers, in which case at Art's death distributions will be spread over the life expectancy of the oldest of Art's grandchildren. Or Art could divide his IRA up into six equal IRAs naming a grandchild as the beneficiary of each. This way at Art's death each of the little Dodgers could use his or her life expectancy.

WAIT AND SEE

No one, not even Art, knows what the future may bring. Art is, therefore, in a dither over whether he should name Ellie, his bypass trust, or Roger as the beneficiary of his IRA. Art can "copper his bets" by naming Ellie as his first beneficiary, the bypass trust as his second beneficiary, and Roger as his third beneficiary. If, at Art's death, there are not enough assets to fund the bypass trust, Ellie can disclaim whatever portion of the IRA is necessary to top it off. Or if it makes sense for Roger to have the IRA, Ellie can disclaim the IRA both individually and as trustee of the bypass trust. Roger will thus become the beneficiary of the IRA just as if Art had named him in the first place.

PAYING ESTATE TAXES OUT OF NON-IRA ASSETS

On Art's death if estate taxes can be paid out of non-IRA assets, the entire IRA can continue to compound free of income taxes. Although not always economically feasible, life insurance can sometimes provide the cash necessary to pay estate taxes so the IRA can be kept intact.

SPLITTING UP THE IRA

If Art names a QTIP trust as beneficiary, not only can Art not use Roger's life expectancy, but also Roger must wait for Ellie's death before he receives the first nickel. What if, instead, Art split his IRA in half, for example, naming Ellie as the beneficiary of one half and Roger as the beneficiary of the other? That way on Art's death, Ellie can roll her IRA over and can take from it whatever she needs. And Roger can immediately begin receiving distributions that can be stretched out over his life expectancy.

GIFTS TO CHARITY

We know that Art is not charitably disposed, but Ellie is. If Ellie wants to leave something to her favorite charity, why not name the charity as the beneficiary of her $100,000 IRA. At her death, her IRA escapes not only estate tax but also income tax. The charity receives 100% of the IRA, and Uncle Sam not a farthing. Or if Ellie wants to provide for Roger, she can name a charitable remainder trust (see chapter 15) as her beneficiary. At Ellie's death Roger receives annual payments from the trust during his lifetime, but at his death the balance passes to charity. Ellie must be careful, however. Only the charitable portion of Ellie's IRA escapes tax at her death, and the IRA, since it passes into a charitable trust, is not available for the payment of the taxes on Roger's lifetime interest. Therefore, Ellie must make sure there are sufficient assets in the rest of her estate to pay the balance of the estate tax.

ROTH IRA

In 1998 Uncle Sam heard a rumor that a group of Stanford professors, working around the clock in a secret underground library, were actually beginning to understand how IRAs work. "Not on my watch," he declared, and he set about inventing the Roth IRA, which reverses almost all the rules.

For example:

- Art *cannot* deduct his contributions to the Roth IRA, but
- He *can* take distributions out tax free, and
- He can withdraw as *much* or as *little* as he wants *without* penalty.

If Art's income is below a certain level, he can either contribute annually to a Roth IRA or roll all or part of his existing IRA into a Roth IRA.

The advantage of a Roth IRA is that although Art pays a tax up front, what is left compounds tax free and is eventually distributed tax free. If given enough time to grow, Roth IRAs can produce dramatic income tax savings.

EDUCATIONAL IRA

In 1998 Uncle Sam also invented the educational IRA. For example, Art can contribute up to $500 each year to an educational trust for each of the six little Dodgers who is under age 18. Like the Roth IRA, contributions to the educational IRA are not deductible, but distributions for higher education expenses come out tax free. Also, like the Roth IRA the educational IRA is limited to individuals with incomes below a certain level.

Do you own life insurance? Maybe you shouldn't. To find out, read on.

Life Insurance: Get Rid of It

Let's talk about life insurance. Wait! Don't turn the page! I am not trying to sell you anything. There are things you must know about life insurance if you are serious about saving taxes. So read on.

YES, IT'S TAXABLE

Years ago the Artful Dodger purchased a $100,000 policy of life insurance naming his son, Roger, as the beneficiary. Art is the owner of the policy. He is also the insured, since it is his death that will trigger the payoff of $100,000. Roger, as the beneficiary, will get the money.

Art is shocked to discover that on his death the $100,000 will be taxed in his estate. What is especially galling to Art is that he purchased life insurance to pay estate taxes, not to create them. In addition to a couple of Valium, Art needs some basic tax advice.

THE SOLUTION

There is a simple solution to Art's problem: Art should give the insurance policy to Roger. Art will still be the insured and Roger will still be the beneficiary. Only the ownership of the policy will change.

"Do you mean to tell me that insurance on my life can be owned by someone other than me?" Art asks. Absolutely.

"Isn't that a taxable gift?" Art persists. Probably not. Though the proceeds from the policy at Art's death will be $100,000, the policy's value while Art is alive is relatively small. If it is under $10,000, Art can give the policy to Roger tax free under the annual exclusion. (Remember the annual exclusion?) Together, Art and his wife can give Roger an insurance policy worth $20,000 tax free.

Now for the really exciting news! At Art's death, since Art no longer owns the life insurance the $100,000 will pass to Roger tax free, that is, free of estate tax and free of income tax.

BUT BE CAREFUL

"So what's the hitch?" asks Art, who has been on guard ever since he lost his shirt in a tax shelter having something to do with recycling used dental floss. Only two hitches: First, Art must survive the gift by three years or the entire $100,000 will be taxed in his estate. Second, Roger, not Art, should pay future insurance premiums or some of the $100,000 will be taxed in Art's estate. (Art, however, can give Roger the money to pay the premiums.)

A BETTER SOLUTION

Art can go one step further. He can name Roger's children as beneficiaries and then give the policy to the children. In this way he can transfer $100,000 to his grandchildren tax free. The $100,000 is thus taxed in neither Art's nor Roger's estate. This may present a problem if there is a chance Roger's children will cash in the policy the first time they walk past a store window displaying roller blades.

As you know from reading chapter 9, Art can solve this problem by transferring the policy to the trustee of an irrevocable trust or to a custodian under the Uniform Transfers to

Minors Act who will administer the insurance proceeds on Art's death for the benefit of the grandchildren.

In most cases, transferring ownership of insurance policies can be accomplished easily and without the need of a lot of high-priced legal talent. In fact, a call to your insurance agent is usually all it takes to obtain the forms necessary to make the change. And the tax savings can be dramatic!

In the next chapter we are going to travel to some pretty exotic islands. The question is, should we take all our earthly possessions with us?

CHAPTER 29

Go Offshore, Young Man

Our favorite worrywart, the Artful Dodger, has been losing sleep, not to mention hair, lately. Now that he has scads of money, he is obsessed by the idea that someone, besides Uncle Sam, will try to take it away from him. Art has read about juries awarding great gobbets of cash for injuries not much worse than a hangnail. Lately, in the watch hours of the morning, he's had dark visions of his home being sold at sheriff's auction, of his tanning booth being repossessed.

Art was, therefore, all ears when a golfing buddy boasted that he, along with all of the other "smart-money" guys, had "gone offshore" with their assets.

Art immediately rushed off to his Clever Attorney to see if he too could join the ranks of the smart-money guys.

GOING OFFSHORE

Indeed, so-called foreign protection of assets trusts have generated much interest lately. So much so that a latter-day Horace Greeley might be heard to say, "Go offshore, young man, go offshore." For which one of us isn't beguiled by the dream of sitting on a beach next to a stack of hard-earned dollars, watching our creditors pile up on the reef? Unfortunately, as Art learned, for most of us the dream may have a morning after.

The idea of an offshore trust is simple. The grantor creates a trust under the laws of a foreign country and then transfers his or her assets into the trust. The trust makes distributions to family members such as his or her spouse and their children. At the end of the term of the trust, the grantor can either take the assets back or, if creditors are still lurking, extend the trust.

FRAUDULENT CONVEYANCES

The trust does not save taxes. Its sole objective is to protect assets from creditors. But creditors have protections, too.

For example, a transfer to an offshore trust cannot be a fraudulent conveyance. In 1571, the Statute of Elizabeth declared void all transfers of property made with the intent of defrauding creditors. The U.S. and many other countries have similar statutes. The offshore trust must be established under the laws of a foreign country that recognizes trusts but that isn't overly bothered by the Statute of Elizabeth. Currently some of these countries are the Bahamas, the Cayman Islands, the Cook Islands, Cyprus, and Gibralter.

Nonetheless, the grantor should also be concerned with the fraudulent conveyance laws here at home. Some grantors smugly assume that any U.S. judgment against them based on a fraudulent conveyance will be unenforceable in the foreign country of their trust. This may be, but assets such as the family residence remaining in the U.S. are still subject to creditors' claims. Moreover, the grantor might be subject to criminal penalties.

Offshore trusts also create problems for the attorney. For whom do you think the creditors will chase when they discover that the grantor's assets have all gone on an island vacation? Perhaps the solution is that no attorney should draft an offshore trust who doesn't have one of his or her own.

Offshore trusts tend to be expensive. They can cost more than $15,000 to set up and $5,000 or more per year thereafter.

On balance, offshore trusts raise significant legal, financial, and ethical questions. For a few the offshore trust may be a panacea; but for the rest of us it will remain a dream.

THE ALASKAN TRUST

A few years ago a bunch of Clever Alaskan Attorneys were tossing a few back with some members of the Fairbanks chamber of commerce. The chamber folks were complaining about the difficulty of attracting tourists to Alaska during the winter season, which runs roughly from August 15 to July 15. The Alaskan attorneys were complaining about the really Clever Attorneys in the Bahamas, the Cayman Islands, the Cook Islands, Cyprus, and Gibralter who were making satchels of money from offshore trusts. Somebody, no one can remember who, said something about opportunity being the twin sister of adversity, and before you could say "aurora borealis," the Alaskan trust was born.

The Alaskan trust

(1) Is irrevocable,

(2) Allows distributions to be made to you,

(3) Can last as long as you want, and

(4) Most importantly, it is free from the claims of creditors that arise *after* you set it up.

Of course, you must hire one of those Clever Alaskan Attorneys to draft the trust and an Alaskan trust company to manage it, which is not cheap. Since the invention of the Alaskan trust, other states that also have severe winters, such as Delaware, Idaho, Illinois, South Dakota, and Wisconsin, are rushing to copy Alaska's "creditor proof" trusts.

Next we will look at some less exotic, more traditional ways of keeping creditors at bay.

Protecting Your Booty

When we last saw the Artful Dodger, he was in a state of acute paranoia over the prospect of hordes of creditors swooping down to plunder his precious possessions. (This is highly unlikely since Art is the type of person who rushes down to pay his monthly utility bill in person and has receipts to prove it going back to the Great Depression.) Having reluctantly decided to pass on the offshore trust and the Alaskan trust, Art is casting about for more conventional ways to preserve wealth. So he dropped by his Clever Attorney's office to have a chat.

EXEMPT ASSETS

First off, under state law even the most rapacious creditor cannot grab certain assets. The states have widely varying exemption laws. For example, in California, Art, having reached the age of 65, finds that he and Ellie have a homestead exemption of $100,000. This means that up to $100,000 of equity in the family residence is secure. (Art's son, Roger, and his wife, because neither is 65, have an exemption of $75,000.) If the Dodger's lived in Texas, they would have an unlimited homestead exemption. But if they lived in New York, their homestead exemption would be a paltry $10,000.

Most states also exempt, for example, automobiles, household furnishings and personal effects, jewelry and works of art, life insurance policies, and certain retirement benefits.

However, most of these exemptions are limited to a modest value.

Although state exemptions are nice to have around, they are so limited that they provide little comfort to most of us.

LIVING TRUSTS

Forget living trusts as a means of protecting assets. At best, a living trust may slow but will not stop the onslaught of creditors.

TAX-SAVING TRUSTS

Perhaps you recall the various tax-saving trusts Art can set up for Ellie: the bypass trust that escapes tax in Ellie's estate, and the QTIP trust that qualifies for the marital deduction (or the qualified domestic trust, if the surviving spouse is not a U.S. citizen).

Each of these trusts, if properly drafted, contains a spendthrift provision. This provision states that the trust is exempt from the claims of the beneficiary's creditors. Thus, Art can place assets that will be secure in trust for the benefit of Ellie. Creditors can only look longingly at these trust assets, much as Aesop's fox looked at the hanging grapes.

CHARITABLE TRUSTS

In chapter 15 we discussed the tax advantages of Art's creating a charitable remainder trust. A charitable remainder trust also gives Art protection against creditors. The assets in the hands of the charity cannot be touched. Art's creditors can, however, reach trust distributions after Art has received them. If Art doesn't like the idea of creditors swooping down on these distributions, he can instruct the trustee to invest solely in growth stock. Then there will be no distributions upon which to swoop. And Art can delay receiving further distribution until his financial troubles have blown over.

All of this makes Art feel somewhat more secure. But at night, on his headboard, the black crows of worry still roost. Perhaps in the next chapter we can put a few of these birds to flight.

CHAPTER 31

Protecting More of Your Booty

Recently, the Artful Dodger's spirits have been on the rise. He now knows creditors can't reach the money he will receive from his charitable trust. Moreover, at his death the property he leaves in trust to his wife, Ellie, also will be protected. To the annoyance of everyone around him, Art has taken to singing, under his breath, over and over again, "Oh, no, they can't take that away from me." Eager to learn more about asset protection, Art wandered back into his Clever Attorney's office to find out more about protecting his booty.

GENERATION-SKIPPING TRUSTS

In estate planning, Art can do for his son, Roger, what Art cannot do for himself. For example, Art cannot protect his property from his creditors' claims merely by creating a living trust. Art can, however, give Roger property in trust either during Art's life or at death. If the trust contains a spendthrift clause, the property will be outside the reach of Roger's creditors. Moreover this trust can continue on for the benefit of the little Dodgers after Roger's death.

As we discussed chapter 5, the primary purpose of such a trust is to pass Art's property to his grandchildren (Roger's children) without its being taxed in Roger's estate. That the property can pass free of creditors' claims as well is an added bonus.

Art must bear in mind that once the assets of a trust are distributed to a beneficiary, they are no longer protected. Art may decide, therefore, to put a "sprinkling power" in his trust. This allows the trustee to choose to which of Art's family members to make distributions. Thus, the trustee can choose *not* to make distributions to a child or grandchild whose creditors are camped out on the welcome mat.

GIFTS TO SPOUSE

Years ago Art, quite foolishly, became a general partner with his son, Roger, in one of Roger's ill-begotten plans to get rich quick. Though nothing bad has happened yet, Art feels it is only a matter of time before Roger's idiot scheme puts him at personal risk. Art has heard of people, especially professionals, giving their property to a spouse to avoid the claims of potential creditors.

Does this scheme work? Possibly. As we have seen, Art can give Ellie any amount, tax free. But the gift must not be a fraud on creditors. Also the gift must be irrevocable and cannot be a mere sham. In other words, no crossed-fingers-behind-the-back stuff.

There is one obvious problem. If Ellie ever gets really fed up with Art (and who could blame her?) and divorces him, Ellie gets to keep all the property. And all Art will end up with is Medicaid eligibility.

Transfers of life insurance involve less risk to Art. He can transfer the ownership of life insurance, naming Ellie as the beneficiary, to her, thereby placing both the policy and its proceeds beyond the reach of his creditors. If Art and Ellie do part company, all Art will have lost is the cash surrender value of the policy.

CORPORATIONS AND
PARTNERSHIPS

Always eager to make more money, Art, in his spare time, has invented a fully biodegradable beer can. Art worries about the liability he might incur if his invention doesn't work out just right. (Several cans, for example, have biodegraded prematurely, leaving a mess in Ellie's refrigerator.)

By incorporating his venture Art can probably limit his liability to the assets of the corporation. A corporation can be fairly simple. In fact, Art may be able to act as sole shareholder, director, and officer.

An alternative to a corporation is the limited liability company (LLC), which is available in many states. The LLC is taxed like a partnership (which is simpler than a corporation), yet it affords the same protection from liability as a corporation.

INSURING AGAINST
THE RISK

Many of the most serious risks Art faces, such as those involving personal injury or property damage, are covered by insurance Art has purchased on his home, car, and business. Of course, Art should periodically review these policies to make sure he is adequately protected. He should also consider buying an umbrella policy, which increases the protection afforded by all these policies. Since an umbrella policy only supplements existing insurance, it is surprisingly affordable.

In the next chapter we will explore the question, "Do you need a conservatorship?" Hint: If you think you do, you probably don't.

If You Think You Do,
You Probably Don't

One day the Artful Dodger and his wife, Ellie, dropped in on their Clever Attorney to discuss estate planning. While Art was out wiping the chalk mark off the tire of his Geo Metro, Ellie told the Clever Attorney about something that had been bothering her. At least once a day, Ellie confided, she walks into a room to get something and ends up standing in the middle of the room without any idea why she is there. "Perhaps I should know something about conservatorships," Ellie said, smiling weakly.

Two thoughts popped into the Clever Attorney's head. The first thought he disclosed to Ellie. It was that people who think they may need a conservatorship, generally don't; and people who don't, often do.

The second thought he kept to himself. It was that he had the same problem as Ellie. Only it happened to him several times each day.

Even though not a candidate for a conservatorship, Ellie wanted to know more about it.

SOME DEFINITIONS

A conservatorship is a court proceeding to take care of people who cannot take care of themselves or who might fall prey to the undue influence of others. A person does not have to be incompetent to have a conservatorship. In fact, a person who is competent can petition for the appointment of a conservator for himself or herself.

First, let's get the nomenclature out of the way. The person under a disability is the conservatee. The person charged with the responsibility of caring for the conservatee is the conservator. (As you Gilbert and Sullivan fans know, in the case of a minor the parties are known as the ward and the guardian, respectively.)

The conservator of the estate manages the conservatee's property. The conservator of the person manages the conservatee's personal care. This can be the same person.

THE PROCEDURE

The laws governing conservatorships vary from state to state. Here is a description of how a typical conservatorship works.

The court proceeding is started when a petition for the appointment of a conservator is filed by an interested party. Unless the petition is filed by the proposed conservatee, the proposed conservatee must be served with a citation advising him or her of the petition and the hearing date and ordering him or her to attend.

Our judicial system zealously protects the rights of incapacitated people, so much so that some judges have their own investigators who independently apprise them of a conservatee's situation. After the petition is filed, the court investigator interviews the proposed conservatee and files a comprehensive report describing the conservatee's condition. The investigator asks the conservatee if he or she wants the conservatorship and if he or she approves of the proposed conservator. The investigator also makes recommendations as to the need for the conservatorship and the appropriate level of care.

Unless unwilling or physically unable, the proposed conservatee attends the hearing. The judge may question the proposed conservator and conservatee to ensure the appointment is appropriate. If the proposed conservatee objects to being conserved, the court appoints an attorney to represent his or her interests and sets the matter for further hearing. If the proposed conservatee makes no objection and the court finds it is in his or her best interests, a conservator is appointed and letters of conservatorship issue. These letters give the conservator authority to act on the conservatee's behalf.

In the next chapter we will see how conservatorships can be used to do some crucial estate planning for individuals who, due to their incapacity, can't do it themselves.

CHAPTER 33

Doing for Others . . .

When we wound up the last chapter, the conservator had just been appointed and letters of conservatorship had issued.

THE BOND

Unless the conservatee is competent and waives it, the court will require the conservator to post a bond. In some states, for example, the amount of the bond is equal to the value of the personal property of the estate plus the estimated annual income earned by those assets. For example, if the conservatorship assets (exclusive of real property) total $500,000, the bond will be set at $525,000, assuming an annual income of 5%. The cost of this bond can range from $600 to $1,200 or more per year.

Think of a bond as an insurance policy that protects the conservatorship estate from loss if the conservator goes "over the hill" with the conservatorship assets. The amount of the bond sometimes can be reduced to the extent assets are deposited in a blocked bank account and receipts are filed with the court.

THE INVENTORY AND APPRAISAL

The conscientious reader of this book will no doubt have noticed the similarity between conservatorship and probate proceedings. (The rest of you really should pay closer attention.) As in the case of probate, the conservator files an inventory with the court, listing all conservatorship assets. These assets are appraised by a court-appointed referee.

COURT REPORTS

Periodically (usually every year or two), the conservator files with the court a report that must include a balanced accounting.

The conservator is entitled to a fee that the judge must approve. This fee is usually based on the hours spent handling the conservatorship. Judges are scrutinous of these fees and may reduce the fees requested by the conservator or by the conservator's attorney if they are not substantiated. If the conservator is a family member, he or she often waives any fee.

Some important actions of the conservator, such as selling the conservatee's residence, require advance court approval. Before deciding the matter, the judge may order the court investigator to visit the conservatee and advise the judge of the conservatee's wishes and ability to remain in the residence.

IT'S NEVER TOO LATE

A conservator can even petition the court to do estate planning for the conservatee. By this procedure, the court and the conservator can accomplish some of those things the conservatee probably would want to do himself or herself.

Take the case of the Artful Dodger's Aunt Dottie, who is mentally incompetent. Aunt Dottie never got around to doing much in the way of estate planning. Now she lacks the capacity to write a will, create a trust, or make gifts. As a result, unless something is done, unnecessary estate taxes and administration expenses will be incurred at her death.

In times past, Aunt Dottie's conservator could do little more than wring his or her hands. Today, however, in most states the conservator can petition the court to do many of the things Aunt Dottie could have done were she competent.

For example, Aunt Dottie was in the habit of giving her children annual gifts of $10,000. Aunt Dottie's conservator can seek court approval to continue making the gifts on her behalf, thus reducing the size of her taxable estate.

The court can also authorize the conservator to set up a living trust for Aunt Dottie to avoid probate, or to change Aunt Dottie's estate plan to save estate taxes.

As you already know, an alternative to a conservatorship is a living trust, which many find attractive because it usually requires no court involvement. One important limitation of the living trust, however, is that the trustee, unlike the conservator, is not permitted to do estate planning for someone like Aunt Dottie.

In the next chapter you will get an entirely biased view of how to pick your own Clever Attorney.

34

Choosing Your Own Clever Attorney

Now that you know something about estate planning, you just might want to find your own Clever Attorney to put some of these concepts to work for you. Here are some thoughts on how you might go about this.

REFERRALS

There is no better way to choose an attorney than to profit from someone else's experience. Ask around among your friends, your accountant, your banker, your analyst. Chances are, before long the names of one or two attorneys will come up over and over again.

If you have had a good experience with an attorney in the past (I know what you're thinking), the obvious place to start is with him or her. Be sure to ask if estate planning is one of his or her specialties. If not, this attorney probably knows the territory and can refer you to someone local who is well regarded professionally.

ADVERTISING

I must warn you that what follows is an entirely biased opinion on the subject of legal advertising: When it comes to choosing an attorney from the Yellow Pages, my advice is, "Let your fingers take a rest." It is simply not true that the size of an ad is inversely proportional to the competency of the attorney. But neither is it any guaranty that the attorney who

placed the ad is well qualified. You should no more
pick your attorney on the
basis of advertising than you
would your family doctor.

At one time attorneys were ethically forbidden to adver-
tise. Now, the floodgates are open, and tasteless, sometimes
downright misleading ads abound, not only in the Yellow
Pages but throughout the media as well. When an attorney
tells you in boldface type how wonderful he or she is, take it
with a grain of salt.

The Yellow Pages can serve one useful purpose. At the
end of all that advertising, look for an "Attorney Guide" listing lawyers who hold themselves out as practicing in various fields. For an estate planning attorney, look under
"Wills, Trusts, and Estate Planning." This guide at least tells
you the attorney's own characterization of his or her area of
expertise.

CERTIFICATION

Some state bar associations certify attorneys who have demonstrated proficiency in certain fields. Probate, Estate Planning, and Trusts is one such field. Taxation is another. To become a specialist, an attorney must pass an examination in his or her chosen specialty and then demonstrate both experience and special training in that field. Although some competent estate planners are not certified, certification is one more factor to weigh in your decision.

PEER REVIEW

A national directory of lawyers (known as the *Martindale-Hubbell Law Directory*) is available at most public libraries. Here you can find out, among other things, where an attorney went to school, when he or she was graduated, the type of clientele he or she represents, and the area of his or her practice.

More importantly, you will see how fellow attorneys rate both an attorney's ethics and competency. *Martindale-Hubbell* goes to great lengths to obtain a fair consensus of an attorney's reputation from among his or her peers. As a result, attorneys often rely on these ratings when making referrals. Don't overlook this valuable source of information.

Now that you know how to find your own Clever Attorney, let's see how you can assist in preparing the estate plan that's right for you—and for the right price.

Preparing for Your Own
Clever Attorney

Years ago, Art learned in high school physics that there are
certain immutable laws of cause and effect. To his dismay, the
same immutable laws apply every time he ventures into his
Clever Attorney's office to discuss his estate plan—for the
predictable effect of each visit is a bill. Here are some suggestions that will reduce the time (not to mention the bill) you
(and Art) would otherwise spend with your attorney devel-
oping your estate plan.

THE FACTS

Most estate-planning attorneys have clients fill out a questionnaire listing assets and liabilities. If possible, get a copy of
this questionnaire, fill it out, and drop it off at your attorney's
office before your first conference.

If your attorney doesn't have a questionnaire, make up
your own financial statement. Better yet, if you have your personal finances on a computer, run off a statement of assets
and liabilities. Be sure to state exactly how each asset is titled.
And don't forget to list all retirement plans along with life insurance policies.

You should also prepare a list of the names and addresses
of members of your immediate family, in addition to those
persons you named in your will (or trust) as beneficiaries or
personal representatives (trustees). In large families it is helpful to diagram your family tree, showing the relationships of

your nearest relatives. Remember to list relatives who have died leaving children.

Even if you are not giving a farthing to your relatives, your attorney will need this information. At your death the law requires that your heirs be notified even if you disinherited them. This is not out of a misguided sense of fun but rather to give all interested parties notice of a probate or trust proceeding in case they wish to contest it. (Appendices K and L are sample Confidential Client Questionnaires, containing financial and family information that you may find useful.)

THE DOCUMENTS

Your attorney will want to review certain documents that are important in preparing your estate plan. Don't forget to bring copies of the following to your first meeting:

- Deeds to real property. If you can't find a deed, the local title company will obtain a copy, usually at no charge, if you provide the assessor's parcel number.
- Life insurance policies, with all change-of-beneficiary forms.
- Buy-sell, partnership, and other agreements relating to any business you own.
- Beneficiary designation statements for all retirement assets (like IRAs and Keogh plans).
- Your existing estate planning documents.

BONING UP

Estate planning has become very complex. Your attorney must try to explain, in a short time, complicated estate planning concepts that took him several semesters in law school to master. Moreover, the attorney who can communicate in plain English has yet to be born. It is no wonder, therefore, that most clients' eyes start to glaze over three minutes into a discussion of QTIP trusts.

The more you already know about the general concepts of estate planning, the better you will understand what your attorney is trying to tell you. And the less time he or she will spend in explanation. It is well worth your time, therefore, to spend a few hours boning up in advance. This knowledge is not hard to come by.

Every bookstore has a legal section with shelves groaning under the weight of estate planning books written for the non-lawyer. I shamelessly hasten to add that this little book is not a bad place to start. And to reward those of you who have stuck it out this far, I have included crib notes for you (Appendix M), summarizing some of the techniques we have discussed. Feel free to take this checklist with you when you next visit your Clever Attorney.

By following these simple suggestions you will enter your attorney's office with an air of sang-froid, prepared to help him or her prepare the estate plan that is right for you.

In the next chapter we will look as some questions you might just want to discuss with your Clever Attorney.

CHAPTER 36

Questions to Ask
Your Own Clever Attorney

Nobody, not even the Artful Dodger's Clever Attorney, is perfect. In fact, just the other day Art's Clever Attorney discovered he had screwed up.

WHO SHOULD PAY ESTATE TAXES?

For years Art's Aunt Agatha has lived in a little cottage Art and Ellie own. Since Agatha is as poor as a church mouse, Art and Ellie have willed the cottage to her so that, if she survives them, she will always have a place to live. The Dodgers' wills did not state on whom the burden of estate taxes would fall. As a result, taxes would be prorated among all beneficiaries, and poor Aunt Agatha would have to sell the cottage to pay her share.

Fortunately, this problem was discovered by the Clever Attorney during a routine review of the Dodgers' estate file. Before his second cup of coffee, he was on the phone to the Dodgers suggesting their wills be changed so the cottage will pass to Agatha free of tax.

The point is simple: Be sure to discuss with your attorney just where you want the burden of taxes to fall.

Estate planning requires detailed fact-gathering. Even the cleverest attorney, on occasion, fails to ask questions, such as this one, that are crucial to an estate plan. Here are some other occasionally overlooked questions you just might want to discuss with your Clever Attorney.

WHAT IF MY CHILD DIES FIRST?

Art and Ellie have willed most of their estate to their son, Roger. If Roger dies before they do, their estate passes to Roger's children. The Dodgers' wills read this way because that is the way the standard will in their Clever Attorney's word processor reads. But what of Roger's widow? If the vision of the little Dodgers sitting around the table eating smoked salmon while their mother eats canned tuna is disturbing, Art and Ellie may just want to give some of their estate to Roger's widow, who, after all, will have the responsibility of raising their grandchildren.

HOW SHOULD I DISPOSE OF FAMILY HEIRLOOMS?

If Art and Ellie had more than one child, like most folks they would probably leave their family heirlooms, memorabilia, jewelry, and the like to their children equally. This often sows the seeds of future sibling warfare. ("Mother said *I* could have Aunt Mildred's milking stool.") It is usually not practical to list heirlooms item by item in your will. Ask your attorney about other ways to distribute these assets. For example, you can tag heirlooms with the children's initials. Or attach a letter with specific instructions to your will or trust. Or, if the kids can't agree, designate just how the property can be divided by lot and designate someone outside the family (who, incidentally, will never forgive you) to preside over the division.

SHOULD I GIVE MY SPOUSE THE RIGHT TO DECIDE WHO WILL INHERIT MY ESTATE?

If Art wills his property to Ellie, in trust, he must state what will happen to the property on Ellie's death. Instead of requiring that his estate pass to Roger, Art can give Ellie the right, during her lifetime, to choose how Art's estate ultimately will be distributed among Roger and the little Dodgers. This is called a limited power of appointment.

If Roger doesn't need any more money, Ellie could leave Art's estate to Roger's children instead. And Ellie could choose which of her grandchildren should inherit. For example, she could leave a healthy amount to the grandchild who is selflessly teaching disabled children and little or nothing to the grandchild who dropped out of school at 14 to express himself on a Harley-Davidson.

For the finale, I have chosen to reveal the legal equivalent of the secret of the universe when it comes to saving taxes.

CHAPTER 37

The Ultimate Tax Dodge

For purely theatrical reasons, I have saved the best part for last. Here now is the Godzilla of all tax loopholes.

Let's say you are a single person with $1,000,000. You want to take a cruise around the world in the hopes of meeting a single person with $2,000,000. Want to know how to charge at least 37% of your trip on Uncle Sam's Master Card? The answer is simple—take the cruise. Or as the Nike people say, "Just do it."

In Ben Franklin's day, a penny saved was a penny earned. That was before estate taxes. Today it is more accurate to say, a penny saved is a penny taxed.

In all of our labyrinthine tax planning we often overlook the fact that consumption is the ultimate tax dodge. Uncle Sam cannot tax it if it isn't there. The virtues we were taught as children—prudence, moderation, thrift—serve us less well as we get older (at least from the standpoint of estate planning).

You all remember Aesop's fable about the ant and the grasshopper. The ant worked 16-hour days gathering food for the winter. The grasshopper, on the other hand, danced and drank and regaled all his friends with tasteless lawyer jokes. What Aesop didn't tell you was that when the ant died (probably from stress), Uncle Sam made a killing. But when the grasshopper died (probably from a failed liver), Uncle Sam got nothing.

People are either ants or grasshoppers. If you are reading this chapter, you are an ant. The grasshoppers, having no money to worry about, lost interest in this book a long time ago. The problem with you ants is that you can't stop being ants, even when your storerooms are bursting. But you must try.

And, if you are interested, there is an even more advantageous way to spend your money. Why not consider spending it on charity? A charitable gift gives you a double bonus. Not only does the gift escape taxation in your estate, but you also get to deduct it from your current income. If you are in a 37% income tax bracket (both state and federal) and a 50% estate tax bracket, a gift of $1,000 to your favorite charity will cost you only $315. And when you make a gift to charity during your lifetime, you will get the recognition you deserve, now rather than after you are gone.

So whether your consumption takes the form of doing things that give you pleasure or giving money to charity (which also may give you pleasure), Uncle Sam is picking up some of the tab.

One last thought. It is the shared ambition of most of us to reduce our taxes. But we must not forget that a government's ability to tax is at the very base of its ability to survive.

I admit that Uncle Sam's profligacy with our tax dollars at times suggests the need for a conservatorship. He has, however, given us the type of government that has allowed us to accumulate our booty in the first place. So, in the end, perhaps there are worse things you could do than pay some taxes. The Artful Dodger, or course, doesn't agree with this. But Art, as we know, is an especially tough nut.

This is the last chapter because I have pretty much run out of things to say. (It is simply not true that I ran out in chapter 12.) I have enjoyed writing this little book. I hope it helps you, with the help of your own Clever Attorney, create an estate plan that is just right for you. At least, now at cocktail parties, you can let drop mention of QTIPs, QPRTs, or QDOTs with the nonchalance of someone who really knows.

On behalf of myself and the entire Dodger clan, I thank you for your readership.

NOTES

PICKUP TAX STATES

The following states participate in the pickup tax:

Alabama

Alaska

Arizona

Arkansas

California

Colorado

District of Columbia

Florida

Georgia

Hawaii

Idaho

Illinois

Maine

Minnesota

Missouri

Nevada

New Mexico

North Dakota

Oregon

Rhode Island

South Carolina

Texas

Utah

Vermont

Virginia

Washington

West Virginia

Wisconsin

Wyoming

1. WASTING ART'S EXEMPTION

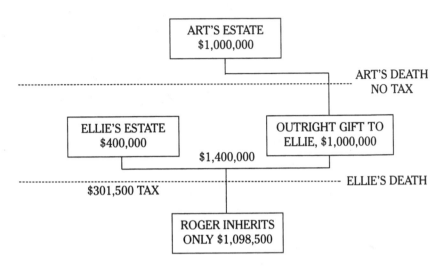

2. GETTING TWO EXEMPTIONS FOR THE PRICE OF ONE

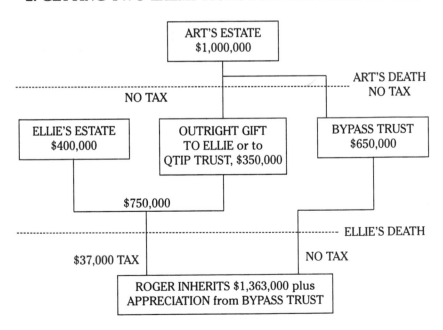

APPENDIX C

THE GENERATION-SKIPPING TRUST

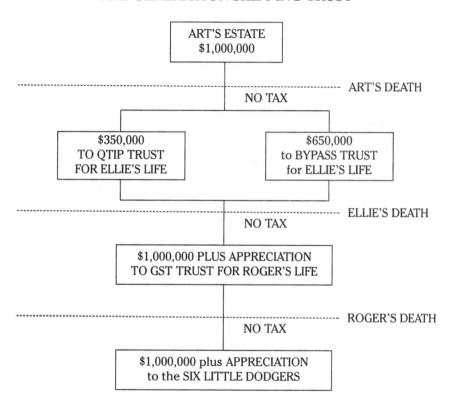

ART'S ESTATE
$1,000,000

------- ART'S DEATH

NO TAX

$350,000
TO QTIP TRUST
FOR ELLIE'S LIFE

$650,000
to BYPASS TRUST
for ELLIE'S LIFE

------- ELLIE'S DEATH

NO TAX

$1,000,000 PLUS APPRECIATION
TO GST TRUST FOR ROGER'S LIFE

------- ROGER'S DEATH

NO TAX

$1,000,000 plus APPRECIATION
to the SIX LITTLE DODGERS

This form is presented by way of example only.
Do not use this form without the advice of your attorney.

ASSIGNMENT OF TANGIBLE
PERSONAL PROPERTY

The undersigned, _____ and _____, hereby assign all right, title, and interest in all tangible items of personal property, all household furniture, furnishings, antiques, art objects, jewelry, precious metals, fine art of every description, and other personal effects whether now owned or hereinafter acquired, in which either party has, or both parties have, an interest, to _____ as Trustee of THE _____ TRUST dated _____, and any amendments made to said trust including those executed after the date of this assignment.

DATED: _____   _____

                                [Husband]

                               _____

                                [Wife]

APPENDIX E

This form is presented by way of example only.
Do not use this form without the advice of your attorney.

DURABLE POWER OF ATTORNEY
FOR HEALTH CARE

[California Probate Code Section 4771]
STATUTORY FORM

WARNING TO PERSON EXECUTING THIS DOCUMENT

THIS IS AN IMPORTANT LEGAL DOCUMENT WHICH IS AUTHORIZED BY THE KEENE HEALTH CARE AGENT ACT. BEFORE EXECUTING THIS DOCUMENT, YOU SHOULD KNOW THESE IMPORTANT FACTS:

1. This document gives the person you designate as your agent (the attorney-in-fact) the power to make health care decisions for you. Your agent must act consistently with your desires as stated in this document or otherwise made known.

2. Except as you otherwise specify in this document, this document gives your agent the power to consent to your doctor not giving treatment or stopping treatment necessary to keep you alive.

3. Notwithstanding this document, you have the right to make medical and other health care decisions for yourself so long as you can give informed consent with respect to the particular decision. In addition, no treatment may be given to you over your objection at the time, and health care necessary to keep you alive may not be stopped or withheld if you object at the time.

4. This document gives your agent authority to consent, to refuse to consent, or to withdraw consent to any care, treatment, service, or procedure to maintain, diagnose, or treat a physical or mental condition. This power is subject to any statement of your desires and any limitations that you include in this document. You may state in this document any types of treatment that you do not desire. In addition, a court can take away the power of your agent to make health care decisions for you if your agent (1) authorizes anything that is illegal, (2) acts contrary to your known desires, or (3) where your desires are not known, does anything that is clearly contrary to your best interests.

5. The powers given by this document will exist for an indefinite period of time unless you limit their duration in this document.

6. You have the right to revoke the authority of your agent by notify-

ing your agent or your treating doctor, hospital, or other health care provider orally or in writing of the revocation.

7. Your agent has the right to examine your medical records and to consent to their disclosure unless you limit this right in this document.

8. Unless you otherwise specify in this document, this document gives your agent the power after you die to authorize an autopsy, donate your body or parts thereof for transplant or therapeutic or educational or scientific purposes, and direct the disposition of your remains.

9. This document revokes any prior durable power of attorney for health care.

10. You should carefully read and follow the witnessing procedure described at the end of this form. This document will not be valid unless you comply with the witnessing procedure.

11. If there is anything in this document that you do not understand, you should ask a lawyer to explain it to you.

12. Your agent may need this document immediately in case of an emergency that requires a decision concerning your health care. Either keep this document where it is immediately available to your agent and alternate agents or give each of them an executed copy of this document. You may also want to give your doctor(s) an executed copy of this document.

13. Do not use this form if you are a conservatee under the Lanterman-Petris-Short Act and you want to appoint your conservator as your agent. You can do that only if the appointment document includes a certificate of your attorney.

1. DESIGNATION OF HEALTH CARE AGENT:

I, _____, do hereby designate and appoint _____, of _____ [Telephone: _____] as my attorney-in-fact to make health care decisions for me as authorized in this document. For the purposes of this document, "health care decisions" means consent, refusal of consent, or withdrawal of consent to any care, treatment, service, or procedure to maintain, diagnose, or treat an individual's physical or mental condition.

2. CREATION OF DURABLE POWER OF ATTORNEY FOR HEALTH CARE:

By this document I intend to create a durable power of attorney for health care under Sections 4600 to 4752, inclusive, of the California Civil Code. This power of attorney is authorized by the Keene Health Care Agent Act and shall be construed in accordance with the provisions of Sections 4770 to 4779, inclusive, of the Probate Code. This power of attorney shall not be affected by my subsequent incapacity.

3. GENERAL STATEMENT OF AUTHORITY GRANTED:

Subject to any limitations in this document, I hereby grant to my agent full power and authority to make health care decisions for me to the same extent that I could make such decisions for myself if I had the capacity to do so. In exercising this authority, my agent shall make health care decisions that are consistent with my desires as stated in this document or otherwise made known to my agent, including, but not limited to, my desires concerning obtaining or refusing or withdrawing life-prolonging care, treatment, services, and procedures.

4. DESIRES, SPECIAL PROVISIONS, AND LIMITATIONS:

[Your agent must make health care decisions that are consistent with your known desires. You can, but are not required to, state your desires in the space provided below. You should consider whether you want to include a statement of your desires concerning life-prolonging care, treatment, services, and procedures. You can also include a statement of your desires concerning other matters relating to your health care. You can also make your desires known to your agent by discussing your desires with your agent or by some other means. If there are any types of treatment that you do not want to be used, you should state them in the space below. If you want to limit in any other way the authority given your agent by this document, you should state the limits in the space below. If you do not state any limits, your agent will have broad powers to make health care decisions for you, except to the extent that there are limits provided by law.]

In exercising the authority under this durable power of attorney for health care, my agent shall act consistently with my desires as stated below and is subject to special provisions and limitations stated below:

(a) Statement of desires concerning life-prolonging care, treatment, services, and procedures: [If you agree with one of these statements, you may initial that statement—READ ALL OF THESE STATEMENTS CAREFULLY BEFORE YOU SELECT ONE TO INITIAL. You can also write your own statement.]

I do not want my life prolonged and I do not want life-sustaining treatment to be provided or continued if the burdens of the treatment outweigh the expected benefits. I want my agent to consider the relief of suffering and the quality as well as the extent of the possible extension of my life in making decisions concerning life-sustaining treatment.

If this statement reflects your desires, initial here:_____

I want my life to be prolonged and I want life-sustaining treatment to be provided unless I am in a coma which my doctors reasonably believe to be irreversible. Once my doctors have reasonably concluded I am in an irreversible coma, I do not want life-sustaining treatment to be provided or continued.

125

If this statement reflects your desires, initial here:_____

    I want my life to be prolonged to the greatest extent possible without regard to my condition, the chances I have for recovery or the cost of the procedures.

If this statement reflects your desires, initial here:_____

    (b) Additional statement of desires, special provisions, and limitations:

_____

_____

[You may attach additional pages if you need more space to complete your statement. If you attach additional pages, you must date and sign **each** of the additional pages at the same time you sign and date this document.]

    5. INSPECTION AND DISCLOSURE OF INFORMATION RELATING TO MY PHYSICAL OR MENTAL HEALTH:

Subject to any limitations set forth elsewhere in this document, my agent has the power and authority to do all of the following:

    (a) Request, review, and receive any information, verbal or written, regarding my physical or mental health, including but not limited to, medical and hospital records.

    (b) Execute on my behalf any releases or other documents that may be required in order to obtain this information.

    (c) Consent to the disclosure of this information.

If you want to limit the authority of your agent to receive and disclose information relating to your health, you must state the limitations in Paragraph 4 ("Statement of Desires, Special Provisions, and Limitations") above.

    6. SIGNING DOCUMENTS, WAIVERS, AND RELEASES:

Where necessary to implement the health care decisions that my agent is authorized by this document to make, my agent has the power and authority to execute on my behalf all of the following:

    (a) Documents titled or purporting to be a "Refusal to Permit Treatment" and "Leaving Hospital Against Medical Advice".

    (b) Any necessary waiver or release from liability required by a hospital or physician.

    7. AUTOPSY; ANATOMICAL GIFTS; DISPOSITION OF REMAINS:

Subject to any limitations in this document, my agent has the power and authority to do all of the following:

    (a) Authorize an autopsy under Health and Safety Code Section 7113.

(b) Make a disposition of a part or parts of my body under the Uniform Anatomical Gift Act.

(c) Direct the disposition of my remains under Health and Safety Code Section 7100.

If you want to limit the authority of your agent to consent to an autopsy, make an anatomical gift, or direct the disposition of your remains, you must state the limitations in Paragraph 4 ("Statement of Desires, Special Provisions, and Limitations") above.

8. DURATION:

[Unless you specify otherwise in the space below, this power of attorney will exist for an indefinite period of time.]

This durable power of attorney for health care expires on _____.

(Fill in this space ONLY if you want to limit
the duration of this power of attorney).

9. DESIGNATION OF ALTERNATE AGENTS:

[You are not required to designate any alternate agents but you may do so. Any alternate agent you designate will be able to make the same health care decisions as the agent you designated in Paragraph 1 above, in the event that your agent is unable or ineligible to act as your agent. If the agent you designated is your spouse, he or she becomes ineligible to act as your agent if your marriage is dissolved.]

If the person designated as my agent in Paragraph 1 is not available or becomes ineligible to act as my agent to make health care decisions for me or loses the mental capacity to make health care decisions for me, or if I revoke that person's appointment or authority to act as my agent to make health care decisions for me, then I designate and appoint the following persons to serve as my agent to make health care decisions for me as authorized in this document, such persons to serve in the order listed below:

First alternative agent:
Address and telephone number:

Second alternative agent:
Address and telephone number:

10. NOMINATION OF CONSERVATOR OF PERSON:

[A conservator of the person may be appointed for you if a court decides that one should be appointed. The conservator is responsible for your physical care, which under some circumstances includes making health care decisions for you. You are not required to nominate a conservator but you may do so. The court will appoint the person you nominate unless that would be contrary to your best interests. You may, but are not required to, nominate as your conservator the same person you named in Paragraph 1 as your health care agent. You can nominate an

---

127

individual as your conservator by completing the space below.]

If a conservator of the person is to be appointed for me, I nominate the following individuals to serve as conservator of the person to serve alone in the order named:

_____

_____

11. PRIOR DESIGNATIONS REVOKED.

I revoke any prior durable power of attorney for health care.

DATE AND SIGNATURE OF PRINCIPAL:

I sign my name to this Statutory Form Durable Power of Attorney for Health Care on _____, at _____, California.

_____
[PRINCIPAL]

[THIS POWER OF ATTORNEY WILL NOT BE VALID UNLESS IT IS SIGNED BY TWO QUALIFIED WITNESSES WHO ARE PRESENT WHEN YOU SIGN OR ACKNOWLEDGE YOUR SIGNATURE. IF YOU HAVE ATTACHED ANY ADDITIONAL PAGES TO THIS FORM, YOU MUST DATE AND SIGN EACH OF THE ADDITIONAL PAGES AT THE SAME TIME YOU DATE AND SIGN THIS POWER OF ATTORNEY.]

STATEMENT OF WITNESSES

[This document must be witnessed by two qualified adult witnesses. None of the following may be used as a witness: (1) a person you designate as your agent or alternate agent, (2) a health care provider, (3) an employee of a health care provider, (4) the operator of a community care facility, (5) an employee of an operator of a community care facility, (6) the operator of a residential care facility for the elderly, or (7) an employee of an operator of a residential care facility for the elderly. At least one of the witnesses shall make the additional declaration set out following the place where the witnesses sign.]

[READ CAREFULLY BEFORE SIGNING. You can sign as a witness only if you personally know the principal or the identity of the principal is proved to you by convincing evidence.]

[To have convincing evidence of the identity of the principal, you must be presented with and reasonably rely on any one or more of the following:

(1) An identification card or driver's license issued by the California Department of Motor Vehicles that is current or has been

issued within five years.

(2) A passport issued by the Department of State of the United States that is current or has been issued within five years.

(3) Any of the following documents if the document is current or has been issued within five years and contains a photograph and description of the person named on it, is signed by the person, and bears a serial or other identifying number:

(a) A passport issued by a state other than California or by a Canadian or Mexican public agency authorized to issue drivers' licenses.

(b) An identification card issued by a state other than California.

(c) A driver's license issued by a state other than California or by a Canadian or Mexican public agency authorized to issue drivers' licenses.

(d) An identification card issued by any branch of the armed forces of the United States.

(4) If the principal is a patient in a skilled nursing facility, a witness who is a patient advocate or ombudsman may rely upon the representations of the administrator or staff of the skilled nursing facility, or of family members, as convincing evidence of the identity of the principal if the patient advocate or ombudsman believes that the presentations provide a reasonable basis for determining the identity of the principal.

I declare under penalty of perjury under the laws of California that the person who signed or acknowledged this document is personally known to me (or proved to me on the basis of convincing evidence) to be the principal, that the principal signed or acknowledged this durable power of attorney for health care in my presence, that the Principal appears to be of sound mind and under no duress, fraud, or undue influence, that I am not the person appointed as agent by this document, and that I am not a health care provider, an employee of a health care provider, the operator of a community care facility, an employee of an operator of a community care facility, the operator of a residential care facility for the elderly, nor an employee of an operator of a residential care facility for the elderly.

Signed on _____, at _____, California.

_____   _____
Witness

_____   _____

Witness   _____

Furthermore, I declare under penalty of perjury under the laws of the State of California, that I am not related to the Principal by blood, marriage, or adoption; and, to the best of my knowledge, that I am not entitled to any part of the estate of the Principal upon the death of the Principal by operation of law or under a will, codicil, or trust now existing or by operation of law.

Dated: _____   _____

                                   Witness

                                   _____

                                   Witness

STATEMENT OF PATIENT ADVOCATE OR OMBUDSMAN

[If you are a patient in a skilled nursing facility, one of the witnesses must be a patient advocate or ombudsman. The following statement is required only if you are a patient in a skilled nursing facility—a health care facility that provides the following basic services: skilled nursing care and supportive care to patients whose primary need is for availability of skilled nursing care on an extended basis. The patient advocate or ombudsman must sign both parts of the "Statement of Witnesses" above **AND** must also sign the following statement.]

I further declare under penalty of perjury under the laws of California that I am a patient advocate or ombudsman as designated by the State Department of Aging and that I am serving as a witness as required by Subdivision (3) of Section 4701 of the Probate Code.

                    Signature: _____

CERTIFICATE OF LAWYER

I am an attorney authorized to practice law in the State of California and the Principal was my client at the time this power of attorney was executed. I have advised my client concerning his or her rights in connection with this power of attorney and the applicable law and the consequences of signing or not signing this power of attorney, and my client, after being so advised, has executed this power of attorney.

I certify under penalty of perjury that the foregoing is true and correct.

Dated: _____   _____

This form is presented by way of example only.
Do not use this form without the advice of your attorney.

STATEMENT OF DESIRES, SPECIAL PROVISIONS, AND LIMITATIONS FOR DURABLE POWER OF ATTORNEY FOR HEALTH CARE

If I develop any incurable, progressive, or degenerative disease stated to be terminal with respect to outcome (not with respect to time) and no cure is available and treatment only prolongs dying, I request that my physician follow my guide regarding life support and life-sustaining intervention listed below. If any desires are not known and life-sustaining or life-support procedures are utilized in an emergency situation, I request that my desires be respected and followed once they are known to my professional care team. I do not want to be kept alive in a vegetative state.

LIFE SUPPORT

	YES	NO	UNCERTAIN
		MY DESIRES	
Pacemaker—any device that substitutes for the normal heartbeat	❑	❑	❑
Peritoneal Dialysis Kidney Dialysis—alternative means of filtering poisons from the body when the kidneys fail	❑	❑	❑
Respirator—a breathing machine attached to a tube inserted into the lungs through the nose or mouth	❑	❑	❑
Cardiopulmonary resuscitation (CPR)—intervention given by man, machine, or drugs when the heart and/or lungs stop working	❑	❑	❑

LIFE-PROLONGING OR LIFE-SUSTAINING PROCEDURES

Feeding tube for food or fluid—a tube placed into the stomach or bowel to give fluid and/or nutrition	❑	❑	❑
Intravenous (IV)—tubes for feeding and hydration	❑	❑	❑

Antibiotics—to treat pneumonia or any other infections	❑	❑	❑
Cancer Therapy—radiation: x-ray treatments given for tumors or cancers; chemotherapy: cancer medicine given by mouth or intravenously	❑	❑	❑
Transfusion—blood or blood products given into the vein	❑	❑	❑
Medical Treatment—diagnostic procedures and tests; further tests and procedures to monitor my failing condition	❑	❑	❑
Surgery—an operation only if it provides for my comfort and dignity	❑	❑	❑
Paramedic—for transport to an acute hospital with CPR in progress	❑	❑	❑
Uniform Gift Act—organ transplant donating body parts; specify parts, if usable	❑	❑	❑
Autopsy—complete or selective, to confirm my diagnosis (check one)	❑	❑	❑

I consent to participate in research, i.e., chemical studies, drug studies, and procedures approved by a Research and Human Subject Review Committee, before or after my death.

Consent may be given by my Attorney-in-Fact	❑	❑	❑

OTHER CONCERNS OR CORRECTIONS

_____

_____

MY WISHES:

1. Caring and supportive nursing and medical care to relieve pain and suffering including narcotics to relieve pain even if respiration is depressed.

2. Food and fluids to be offered as long as I am conscious to take them by mouth and then moist sponges to moisten my lips to relieve the sensation of dehydration.

Signature: _____ Date:_____

This form is presented by way of example only.
Do not use this form without the advice of your attorney.

DIRECTIVE TO PHYSICIANS

[California Health and Safety Code §7186.5]

I, _____, being of sound mind, willfully and voluntarily make known my desire that my life shall not be artificially prolonged under the circumstances set forth below, and I do hereby declare:

If at any time I should have an incurable and irreversible condition that has been diagnosed by two (2) physicians and that will result in my death within a relatively short time without the administration of life-sustaining treatment or has produced an irreversible coma or persistent vegetative state, and I am no longer able to make decisions regarding my medical treatment, I direct my attending physician, pursuant to the Natural Death Act of California, to withhold or withdraw treatment, including artificially administered nutrition and hydration, that only prolongs the process of dying or the irreversible coma or persistent vegetative state and is not necessary for my comfort or to alleviate pain.

If I have been diagnosed as pregnant, and that diagnosis is known to my physician, this declaration shall have no force or effect during my pregnancy.

Signed this _____ day of _____, [Year].

_____
[Signature]
[Address]

The declarant voluntarily signed this writing in my presence. I am not a health care provider, an employee of a health care provider, the operator of a community care facility, am employe of an operator of a community care facility, the operator of a residential care facility for the elderly, or an employee of an operator of a residential care facility for the elderly.

_____   _____
Witness   Address

The declarant voluntarily signed this writing in my presence. I am not entitled to any portion of the estate of the declarant upon his or her death under any will or codicil thereto of the declarant now existing or by operation of law. I am not a health care provider, an employee of a health care provider, the operator of a community care facility, an employee of an operator of a community care facility, the operator of a residential care facility for the elderly, or an employee of an operator of a residential care facility for the elderly

_____

[Witness]
[Address]

APPENDIX

This form is presented by way of example only.
Do not use this form without the advice of your attorney.

UNIFORM STATUTORY FORM POWER OF ATTORNEY—EFFECTIVE IMMEDIATELY

When recorded, return to:

[Name

Address]

UNIFORM STATUTORY FORM
POWER OF ATTORNEY

[California Probate Code §4401]

NOTICE: THE POWERS GRANTED BY THIS DOCUMENT ARE BROAD AND SWEEPING. THEY ARE EXPLAINED IN THE UNIFORM STATUTORY FORM POWER OF ATTORNEY ACT (CALIFORNIA PROBATE CODE SECTIONS 4400–4465). IF YOU HAVE ANY QUESTIONS ABOUT THESE POWERS, OBTAIN COMPETENT LEGAL ADVICE. THIS DOCUMENT DOES NOT AUTHORIZE ANYONE TO MAKE MEDICAL AND OTHER HEALTH-CARE DECISIONS FOR YOU. YOU MAY REVOKE THIS POWER OF ATTORNEY IF YOU LATER WISH TO DO SO.

I, _____, a resident of _____, California, appoint _____ [Name and address of the person appointed or of each person appointed if you want to designate more than one], as my agent (attorney-in-fact) to act for me in any lawful way with respect to the following initialed subjects:

TO GRANT ALL OF THE FOLLOWING POWERS, INITIAL THE LINE IN FRONT OF (P) AND IGNORE THE LINES IN FRONT OF THE OTHER POWERS.

TO GRANT ONE OR MORE, BUT FEWER THAN ALL, OF THE FOLLOWING POWERS, INITIAL THE LINE IN FRONT OF EACH POWER YOU ARE GRANTING.

TO WITHHOLD A POWER, DO NOT INITIAL THE LINE IN FRONT OF IT. YOU MAY, BUT NEED NOT, CROSS OUT EACH POWER WITHHELD.

INITIAL

_____ (A) Real property transactions.

_____ (B) Tangible personal property transactions.

_____ (C) Stock and bond transactions.

_____ (D) Commodity and option transactions.

_____ (E) Banking and other financial institution transactions.

_____ (F) Business operating transactions.

_____ (G) Insurance and annuity transactions.

_____ (H) Estate, trust, and other beneficiary transactions, including the funding of a revocable trust.

_____ (I) Claims and litigation.

_____ (J) Personal and family maintenance.

_____ (K) Benefits from Social Security, Medicare, Medicaid, or other governmental programs, or civil or military service.

_____ (L) Retirement plan transactions.

_____ (M) Tax matters.

_____ (N) To make annual exclusion gifts on my behalf to my issue (including the holder of this power) and to require the Trustee of any revocable trust of which I am the Settlor to make annual exclusion gifts to my issue (including the holder of this power).

_____ (O) To revoke, amend, or withdraw funds from a revocable trust of which the Principal is a Settlor.

_____ (P) ALL OF THE POWERS LISTED ABOVE.

YOU NEED NOT INITIAL ANY OTHER LINES IF YOU INITIAL LINE (P).

SPECIAL INSTRUCTIONS

ON THE FOLLOWING LINES, YOU MAY GIVE SPECIAL INSTRUCTIONS LIMITING OR EXTENDING THE POWERS GRANTED TO YOUR AGENT.

_____

_____

UNLESS YOU DIRECT OTHERWISE ABOVE, THIS POWER OF ATTORNEY IS EFFECTIVE IMMEDIATELY AND WILL CONTINUE UNTIL IT IS RE-VOKED.

This Power of Attorney will continue to be effective even though I become incapacitated.

STRIKE THE PRECEDING SENTENCE IF YOU DO NOT WANT THIS POWER OF ATTORNEY TO CONTINUE IF YOU BECOME INCAPACI-TATED.

EXERCISE OF POWER OF ATTORNEY WHERE
MORE THAN ONE AGENT DESIGNATED

If I have designated more than one agent, the agents are to act [JOINTLY/SEVERALLY].

IF YOU APPOINT MORE THAN ONE AGENT AND YOU WANT EACH AGENT TO BE ABLE TO ACT ALONE WITHOUT THE OTHER AGENT JOINING, WRITE THE WORD "SEPARATELY" IN THE BLANK SPACE ABOVE. IF YOU DO NOT INSERT ANY WORD IN THE BLANK SPACE, OR IF YOU INSERT THE WORD "JOINTLY," THEN ALL OF YOUR AGENTS MUST ACT OR SIGN TOGETHER.

I agree that any third party who receives a copy of this document may act under it. Revocation of the power of attorney is not effective as to a third party until the third party has actual knowledge of the revocation. I agree to indemnify the third party for any claims that arise against the third party because of reliance on this power of attorney.

Signed this ____ day of _____, [Year].

_____

[Your Signature]

Social Security Number:

_____

State of California

County of _____

On _____, before me, [Notary Public], personally appeared _____, personally known to me or proved to me on the basis of satisfactory evidence to be the person whose name is subscribed to the within instrument and acknowledged to me that he/she/they executed the same in his/her/their authorized capacity(ies), and that by his/her/their signature(s) on the instrument the person(s), or the entity upon behalf of which the person(s) acted, executed the instrument.

WITNESS my hand and official seal.

_____

BY ACCEPTING OR ACTING UNDER THE APPOINTMENT, THE AGENT ASSUMES THE FIDUCIARY AND OTHER LEGAL RESPONSIBILITIES OF AN AGENT.

H-2

This form is presented by way of example only.
Do not use this form without the advice of your attorney.

UNIFORM STATUTORY FORM
POWER OF ATTORNEY—EFFECTIVE ON
SUBSEQUENT INCAPACITY

When recorded, return to:

[Name

Address]

UNIFORM STATUTORY FORM
POWER OF ATTORNEY

[California Probate Code §4401]

NOTICE: THE POWERS GRANTED BY THIS DOCUMENT ARE BROAD AND SWEEPING. THEY ARE EXPLAINED IN THE UNIFORM STATUTORY FORM POWER OF ATTORNEY ACT (CALIFORNIA PROBATE CODE SECTIONS 4400–4465). IF YOU HAVE ANY QUESTIONS ABOUT THESE POWERS, OBTAIN COMPETENT LEGAL ADVICE. THIS DOCUMENT DOES NOT AUTHORIZE ANYONE TO MAKE MEDICAL AND OTHER HEALTH-CARE DECISIONS FOR YOU. YOU MAY REVOKE THIS POWER OF ATTORNEY IF YOU LATER WISH TO DO SO.

I, _____, a resident of _____, California, appoint _____ [Name and address of the person appointed, or of each person appointed if you want to designate more than one], as my agent (attorney-in-fact) to act for me in any lawful way with respect to the following initialed subjects:

TO GRANT ALL OF THE FOLLOWING POWERS, INITIAL THE LINE IN FRONT OF (P) AND IGNORE THE LINES IN FRONT OF THE OTHER POWERS.

TO GRANT ONE OR MORE, BUT FEWER THAN ALL, OF THE FOLLOWING POWERS, INITIAL THE LINE IN FRONT OF EACH POWER YOU ARE GRANTING.

TO WITHHOLD A POWER, DO NOT INITIAL THE LINE IN FRONT OF IT. YOU MAY, BUT NEED NOT, CROSS OUT EACH POWER WITHHELD.

INITIAL

_____ (A) Real property transactions.

_____ (B) Tangible personal property transactions.

_____ (C) Stock and bond transactions.

_____ (D) Commodity and option transactions.

_____ (E) Banking and other financial institution transactions.

_____ (F) Business operating transactions.

_____ (G) Insurance and annuity transactions.

_____ (H) Estate, trust, and other beneficiary transactions, including the funding of a revocable trust.

_____ (I) Claims and litigation.

_____ (J) Personal and family maintenance.

_____ (K) Benefits from Social Security, Medicare, Medicaid, or other governmental programs, or civil or military service.

_____ (L) Retirement plan transactions.

_____ (M) Tax matters.

_____ (N) To revoke, amend, or withdraw funds from a revocable trust of which the Principal is a Settlor.

_____ (O) To make annual exclusion gifts on my behalf to my issue.

_____ (P) **ALL OF THE POWERS LISTED ABOVE.**

[YOU NOT NEED INITIAL ANY OTHER LINES IF YOU INITIAL LINE (P).]

THIS DURABLE POWER OF ATTORNEY SHALL BECOME EFFECTIVE ONLY ON MY SUBSEQUENT INCAPACITY.

I will conclusively be deemed incapacitated for the purposes of this instrument when my agent receives a written and signed opinion from a licensed physician, practicing in the area in which I reside, that I am either physically or mentally incapable of managing my own affairs. Said instrument, when received, shall be attached to this document. Third parties may rely on my agent's authority without further evidence of incapacity when this instrument is presented with such a physician's statement attached pursuant to Probate Code §4405.

EXERCISE OF POWER OF ATTORNEY WHERE MORE THAN ONE
AGENT DESIGNATED

If I have designated more than one agent, the agents are to act _____ [JOINTLY/SEPARATELY].

IF YOU APPOINT MORE THAN ONE AGENT AND YOU WANT EACH AGENT TO BE ABLE TO ACT ALONE WITHOUT THE OTHER AGENT JOINING, WRITE THE WORD "SEPARATELY" IN THE BLANK SPACE ABOVE. IF YOU DO NOT INSERT ANY WORD IN THE BLANK SPACE, OR IF YOU INSERT THE WORD "JOINTLY," THEN ALL OF YOUR AGENTS MUST ACT OR SIGN TOGETHER.

I agree that any third party who receives a copy of this document may act under it. Revocation of the power of attorney is not effective as to a third party until the third party has actual knowledge of the revocation. I agree to indemnify the third party for any claims that arise against the third party because of reliance on this power of attorney.

Signed this ____ day of _____, [Year].

_____

[Your signature]

Social Security Number:

_____

State of California

County of

On _____, before me, [Notary Public], personally appeared _____, personally known to me or proved to me on the basis of satisfactory evidence to be the person whose name is subscribed to the within instrument and acknowledged to me that he/she/they executed the same in his/her/their authorized capacity(ies), and that by his/her/their signature(s) on the instrument the person(s), or the entity upon behalf of which the person(s) acted, executed the instrument.

WITNESS my hand and official seal.

_____

BY ACCEPTING OR ACTING UNDER THE APPOINTMENT, THE AGENT ASSUMES THE FIDUCIARY AND OTHER LEGAL RESPONSIBILITIES OF AN AGENT.

APPNDIX

This form is presented by way of example only.
Do not use this form without the advice of your attorney.

COMMUNITY PROPERTY AFFIDAVIT

We, _____ and _____, husband and wife, hereby de-
clare that all of the property which we now hold or hereafter acquire
in our names as joint tenants or tenants in common or which we hold
as Co-Trustees of a living trust of which we are the Settlors that was formerly held in our names as joint tenants or tenants in common is hereby
transmuted by us to community property with the exception of any
bank or savings accounts standing in our names as joint tenants.

EXECUTED this _____ day of ____, [Year], at _____, California.

_____   _____

[Husband]   [Wife]

This form is presented by way of example only.
Do not use this form without the advice of your attorney.

NOMINATION OF CONSERVATOR

I, _____, hereby nominate the following individuals, in the order in which they are named, as the Conservator of my person:

[First Nominee]

[Second Nominee]

I, _____, hereby nominate the following individuals, in the order in which they are named, as the Conservator of my estate:

[First Nominee]

[Second Nominee]

In the event the first nominee fails to qualify or ceases to act as my Conservator, I nominate the second nominee as Conservator to act in his or her stead.

No bond shall be required of any of the above-nominated Conservators.

This Nomination of Conservator hereby revokes all prior nominations.

DATED: _____   _____
                                                      [Declarant]

This form is presented by way of example only.
Do not use this form without the advice of your attorney.

CONFIDENTIAL CLIENT
QUESTIONNAIRE

(ASSET INFORMATION)

NAME: _____ SPOUSE'S NAME: _____

ESTIMATED VALUE OF GROSS ESTATE: _____

ASSETS

A. Real Property

For each parcel of real property owned by you, please attach a copy of the deed and provide the following information:

Address: _____

How Title Held: _____

Estimated Fair Market Value: _____

Present Encumbrance: _____

Name of Lender(s): _____

(Please attach additional sheets if you own more than one parcel of real property).

B. Corporate Securities

[If your securities are held in a brokerage account, you may simply attach a copy of a recent statement.]

Name of Security   Value

_____ $ _____

_____ $ _____

_____ $ _____

How Title Held: _____

Location of Certificates: _____

Name and Address of Stock Broker: _____

_____

C. Cash

Bank Account/Location	*How Held	Approx. Balance
_____	_____	$ _____
_____	_____	$ _____
_____	_____	$ _____
_____	_____	$ _____
_____	_____	$ _____
_____	_____	$ _____
_____	_____	$ _____

*How Bank Accounts Held (i.e., joint tenancy, individually, tenants in common)

D. Life Insurance

For each life insurance policy owned, please provide the following:

Company/Policy No.	Face Value	Beneficiary(ies)	Owner(s)
_____	$ _____	_____	_____
_____		_____	_____
_____	$ _____	_____	_____
_____		_____	_____

E. Personal Property

Please state the approximate value of all tangible personal property owned by you and its location:

_____

Among your tangible personal property, are there any antiques or objects of art? [Yes/No] _____

F. Retirement/Pension Plans

For each retirement, pension, or profit-sharing plan, please state the following:

Employer: _____

Type of Plan: _____

Designated Beneficiary(ies): _____

_____

_____

Name and Address of Plan Administrator: _____

_____

_____

G. Client-Owned Business

    Name: _____ Type: _____

    Other owners: _____

    Is there a buy-sell agreement? _____

H. Partnership Interests

    Name of Partnership: _____

    Names of Other Partners: _____

    _____

I. Unsecured Liabilities (over $2,500)

    Amount Owed   Payee

    $_____   _____

    $_____   _____

J. Other Assets [i.e., interest in lawsuit, copyrights, patents, mineral rights]

_____

_____

_____

K. Safe Deposit Box: _____ Location: _____

    Location of Key: _____

L. Accountant

    Name and address of your accountant and/or tax adviser:

_____

_____

_____

M. Do you have a beneficial interest in a trust? If so, please provide a copy of the trust.

N. Do you expect to inherit property in the foreseeable future? If so, please describe what you expect to inherit and from whom.

O. Have you made gifts of over $10,000 to anyone? If yes, please provide the name of the person, the date of the gift, and the value of the gift.

    Did you file gift tax returns?

P. Please indicate any special burial or funeral instructions you wish your Executor to know about.

This form is presented by way of example only.
Do not use this form without the advice of your attorney.

CONFIDENTIAL CLIENT QUESTIONNAIRE

(FAMILY INFORMATION)

DATED: _____

NAME: _____ SPOUSE'S NAME: _____

HOME ADDRESS: _____

_____

Home Telephone Number: _____ Work: _____

Your Birthdate: _____ Spouse's Birthdate: _____

Your Social Security number: _____

Spouse's Social Security number: _____

Both spouses U. S. citizens? _____ If not, please indicate citizenship:

NAMES OF CHILDREN:
(Include birthdates, marital status, telephone numbers, and addresses)

NAMES OF CHILDREN OF SPOUSE:
(Include birthdates, marital status, telephone numbers, and addresses)

NAMES OF GRANDCHILDREN:
(Include birthdates and addresses, and identify parent)

NAMES OF YOUR PARENTS, IF LIVING: _____

_____

NAMES OF YOUR SPOUSE'S PARENTS, IF LIVING: _____

_____

If you have neither living parents nor children, please give the name, relationship, and address of your next of kin and those of your spouse:

CHECKLIST OF THINGS TO DISCUSS WITH YOUR OWN CLEVER ATTORNEY

1. Should you have a will or a living trust?
2. If you are married, do you need:
   A. A tax savings trust (bypass trust)? (Probably, if the estate of you and your spouse is likely to exceed $650,000.)
   B. A QTIP trust? (Probably, if you want to control what happens to your property after both you and your spouse are gone.)
   C. A special power of appointment? (Probably, if you want to give your spouse the ability to control what happens to your property after your death.)
   D. A QDOT trust? (Probably, if either of you is not a U.S. citizen and either of you has assets worth over $650,000.)
   E. A community property affidavit? (Probably, if you live in a community property state and own appreciated property.)
   F. A durable general power of attorney? (Probably, if you have a living trust or want an inexpensive alternative to a conservatorship in the event of a temporary disability.)
3. If you have children:
   A. How do you want to leave bequests to minor children?
      (1) To a guardian?
      (2) To a trustee?
      (3) To a custodian under the California Uniform Transfers to Minors Act?
   B. Do you want to make annual exclusion gifts to your children? If so, how do you want to leave the gifts?
      (1) To a custodian under the California Uniform Transfers to Minors Act?
      (2) To a minor's trust?
      (3) To a Crummey trust?
   C. Should you establish a qualified personal residence trust? (Possibly, if you don't mind a bit of a gamble.)
4. If you have grandchildren, do you want to create a generation-skipping trust? (Probably, if you are interested in saving your grandchildren taxes.)

5. Should you execute the following documents:

    A.   A durable power of attorney for health care? (Probably, if there is someone to whom you are willing to delegate your health care decisions.)

    B.   A living will? (Probably, if there is no one to whom you are willing to delegate your health care decisions and if you don't want your life artificially prolonged.)

    C.   A nomination of conservator? (Probably, especially if you don't have a living trust.)

6. If you are charitably minded: Should you make gifts of appreciated property to charity? Should you establish, during your life or at death, a charitable remainder trust?

7. If you have an IRA or other retirement plans, you should:

    A.   Review all beneficiary designations.

    B.   Determine whether a Roth IRA is for you.

A SIMPLIFIED GLOSSARY
OF TERMS

Author's Note: Following are nontechnical, nonwindy definitions of the concepts covered in this book. They are accurate as far as they go. But if you really want full-blown, detailed definitions, you should consult *Black's Law Dictionary* or other more definitive legal texts.

Alaskan trust an irrevocable trust, usually for the benefit of the person who set it up, that is exempt from creditors' claims arising after its creation.

Alternate valuation date for estate tax purposes, the date six months after the date of death upon which assets may be valued.

Annual exclusion up to $10,000 you can give away annually to each of any number of people, tax free.

Basis, tax what you paid for an asset (in the case of real property, less depreciation plus any improvements).

Beneficiary, life insurance the person (or entity) who, upon the death of the insured, is entitled to receive the insurance proceeds.

Beneficiary, trust the person(s) entitled to receive distributions from a trust.

Bond a written undertaking by a bonding company to protect the estate from losses resulting from theft by the trustee, conservator, or guardian.

Bypass trust a trust, containing up to the exemption amount ($650,000 in 1999), that escapes tax in the surviving spouse's estate.

Capital gains tax income tax you pay on the gain (the difference between an asset's basis and its sales price) when you sell an asset.

Certification, legal attestation by the state bar association that an attorney has qualified as an expert in a particular field.

Charitable remainder trust a trust, eventually passing to charity, that pays you or your family members a set amount of money each year.

Community property property acquired during your marriage other than by gift or inheritance.

Community property affidavit a document confirming that all property held in the name of you and your spouse is community property.

Conservatee the person for whom a conservatorship is established.

Conservator of the estate the court-appointed person (or entity) having the responsibility for the conservatee's financial affairs.

Conservator of the person the court-appointed person (or entity) having the responsibility for the conservatee's personal care.

Corporation a business entity in which the liability of its shareholders is limited to the value of its assets.

Cristofani trust a variation on the Crummey trust that is sufficiently difficult to explain that you will just have to refer to the end of chapter 9.

Crummey trust a trust, usually established for the benefit of a child, that is not required to terminate when the child reaches age 21.

Directive to physicians a document directed to your doctor stating that you do not want your life artificially prolonged.

Disclaimer a document in which you give up your right to all or part of an inheritance.

Durable power of attorney for health care a document in which you appoint someone to make health care decisions for you in the event you are incapable of doing so.

Durable power of attorney, general a document that survives your incompetency and gives another person the right to conduct your financial affairs.

Educational IRA (Individual Retirement Account) a fund for the education of your children to which contributions are *not* deductible but from which distributions for educational purposes are tax free.

Estate taxes taxes imposed by the federal government at your death based on the value of the property in your estate.

Executor, executrix the person (or entity) appointed by the court to administer your estate.

Exempt assets assets not subject to creditors' claims.

Exemption, federal the value of assets ($650,000 in 1999, increasing to $1,000,000 in 2006) you can give away during your life or at death that is not subject to either gift or estate tax.

Extraordinary fees additional fees charged by the probate attorney, subject to court approval, for services not covered by the probate fee.

Fiscal year a tax year, as distinguished from a calendar year, that can be chosen for income tax purposes after your death.

Fraudulent conveyance a transfer of assets made primarily for the purpose of avoiding creditors' claims.

General partnership a partnership in which all partners are liable for partnership obligations.

Generation-skipping trust a trust into which you put up to $1,000,000 that will pass to your grandchildren without being taxed in your children's estates.

Gift taxes taxes imposed by the federal government on lifetime transfers.

GRAT (grantor retained annuity trust) a trust into which the grantor transfers income-producing property, reserving an income interest for a stated number of years (based on a percentage of the original value of the trust) with the remainder usually passing to his or her children.

GRUT (grantor retained unitrust) a trust into which the grantor transfers income-producing property, reserving an income interest for a stated number of years (based on a percentage of the value of the trust calculated annually) with the remainder usually passing to his or her children.

Gross estate the value of your entire estate undiminished by allowable deductions such as debts or administration expenses.

Guardian of the estate the court-appointed person (or entity) having the responsibility for a minor's financial affairs.

Guardian of the person the court-appointed person (or entity) having the responsibility for a minor's personal care.

Homestead exemption the value of your home protected from creditors' claims.

IRA (Individual Retirement Account) a retirement account to which contributions are tax deductible and from which distributions are taxed.

Insured the person whose death causes insurance proceeds to be payable to a named beneficiary.

Intestate succession the manner in which your estate passes under state law if you die without a will.

Inventory and appraisal the document filed in either a probate, a conservatorship, or a guardianship proceeding that lists and values all assets of the estate.

Investigator, court a county employee, reporting directly to the superior court, who evaluates conservatorships and guardianships.

Joint tenancy a method of holding property in the names of two or more people such that upon the death of one the property passes to the survivor(s).

Limited liability company a business entity that is taxed like a partnership but affords the same protection as a corporation.

Limited partnership a partnership in which the liability of the limited partners is restricted to their investment in the company.

Limited power of appointment the power to direct to whom assets will ultimately pass within a limited class of beneficiaries.

Living trust a trust established primarily for the purpose of avoiding probate that is also used as a substitute for a conservatorship.

Marital deduction, unlimited a deduction for federal gift and estate tax purposes that allows you to make unlimited gifts to your spouse tax free.

Marketability discount a discount in value attributable to an asset's being subject to a buyout agreement.

Martindale-Hubbell Law Directory a periodical that provides information on attorneys.

Medicaid a state and federal program providing nursing home benefits.

Medicare a federal program, run as a part of the Social Security system, providing medical benefits.

Minority discount a discount in value attributable to an asset's not being a controlling interest.

Minor's trust a trust, established for the benefit of a child, that terminates when the child reaches age 21.

Nomination of conservator a document in which you nominate your conservator and, if you choose, waive any bond requirement.

Offshore trust a trust established in a foreign country for the purpose of avoiding creditors' claims.

Pickup tax the portion of your federal estate tax that is payable to the state in which you reside.

Pour-over will a will that distributes your estate to your living trust.

Principal, trust the body of a trust that usually bears interest.

Probate the legal process for the orderly distribution of your estate.

Probate fee the fee, established by law, to which your estate representative and the probate attorney are entitled.

QDOT trust (qualified domestic trust) a trust for the benefit of a noncitizen spouse that qualifies for the unlimited marital deduction.

QPRT trust (qualified personal residence trust) a trust into which the grantor transfers his or her residence, reserving an interest for a stated number of years, with the remainder passing usually to his or her children.

QTIP trust (qualified terminable interest property trust) a trust for the benefit of your spouse that qualifies for the unlimited marital deduction.

Roth IRA (Individual Retirement Account) a retirement account to which contributions are *not* deductible but from which distributions are tax free.

Special needs trust a trust for a disabled person, intended to supplement rather than replace public benefit payments.

Spendthrift provision a trust provision that protects a beneficiary's interest in a trust from creditors' claims.

Sprinkling power the power of a trustee to make discretionary distributions to a class of beneficiaries you designate.

Statute of Elizabeth the first statute declaring transfers in fraud of creditors to be void.

Taxable estate your gross estate less deductions such as debts and administration expenses.

Uniform Transfers to Minors Act legislation providing a simple, inexpensive way to transfer property to a custodian for the benefit of a minor.

Ward a minor for whom a guardianship has been established.

Will a document stating how your property will be disposed of upon your death.

INDEX

ORDER FORM

To order this book, please fill in the information requested and send check or money order to

Linthicum Press
P.O. Box 805
Carmel, CA 93921

QUANTITY	PRICE	TOTAL
_____	$ _____	$ _____
California residents please add sales tax		$ _____
Shipping		$ _____
TOTAL		$ _____

SHIPPING INFORMATION

Name and Address _____

_____

_____

_____

Telephone Number _____

Quantity discount: 1–3 books for $17.95 each
4–10 for $15.95 each
over 10 for $14.95 each

Shipping and handling:
$2.00 for 1 book, each additional book $.50

Or call (831) 624-5339

Visit our Web Site www.thawley.com